Kaplan Publishing are constantly finding new ways to make a difference to your studies and our exciting online resources really do offer something different to students looking for exam success.

This book comes with free MyKaplan online resources so that you can study anytime, anywhere. **This free online resource is not sold separately and is included in the price of the book.**

Having purchased this book, you have access to the following online study materials:

CONTENT	AAT	
	Text	Kit
Electronic version of the book	✓	✓
Progress tests with instant answers	✓	
Mock assessments online	✓	✓
Material updates	✓	✓

D0183193

How to access your online resources

Kaplan Financial students will already have a MyKaplan account and these extra resources will be available to you online. You do not need to register again, as this process was completed when you enrolled. If you are having problems accessing online materials, please ask your course administrator.

If you are not studying with Kaplan and did not purchase your book via a Kaplan website, to unlock your extra online resources please go to www.mykaplan.co.uk/addabook (even if you have set up an account and registered books previously). You will then need to enter the ISBN number (on the title page and back cover) and the unique pass key number contained in the scratch panel below to gain access. You will also be required to enter additional information during this process to set up or confirm your account details.

If you purchased through the Kaplan Publishing website you will automatically receive an e-mail invitation to MyKaplan. Please register your details using this email to gain access to your content. If you do not receive the e-mail or book content, please contact Kaplan Publishing.

Your Code and Information

This code can only be used once for the registration of one book online. This registration and your online content will expire when the final sittings for the examinations covered by this book have taken place. Please allow one hour from the time you submit your book details for us to process your request.

Please scratch the film to access your unique code.

Please be aware that this code is case-sensitive and you will need to include the dashes within the passcode, but not when entering the ISBN.

KAPLAN PUBLISHING

ELEMENTS OF COSTING

STUDY TEXT

Qualifications and Credit Framework

AQ2016

This Study Text supports study for the following AAT qualifications:

AAT Foundation Certificate in Accounting – Level 2

AAT Foundation Diploma in Accounting and Business – Level 2

AAT Foundation Certificate in Bookkeeping – Level 2

AAT Foundation Award in Accounting Software – Level 2

AAT Level 2 Award in Accounting Skills to Run Your Business

AAT Foundation Certificate in Accounting at SCQF – Level 5

British Library Cataloguing-in-Publication Data

A catalogue record for this book is available from the British Library.

Published by
Kaplan Publishing UK
Unit 2, The Business Centre
Molly Millars Lane
Wokingham
Berkshire
RG41 2QZ

ISBN: 978-1-78740-776-3

Printed and bound in Great Britain.

CONTENTS

INTRODUCTION

HOW TO USE THESE MATERIALS

These Kaplan Publishing learning materials have been carefully designed to make your learning experience as easy as possible and to give you the best chance of success in your AAT assessments.

They contain a number of features to help you in the study process.

The sections on the Unit Guide, the Assessment and Study Skills should be read before you commence your studies.

They are designed to familiarise you with the nature and content of the assessment and to give you tips on how best to approach your studies.

STUDY TEXT

This study text has been specially prepared for the revised AAT qualification introduced in September 2016.

It is written in a practical and interactive style:

- key terms and concepts are clearly defined
- all topics are illustrated with practical examples with clearly worked solutions based on sample tasks provided by the AAT in the new examining style
- frequent activities throughout the chapters ensure that what you have learnt is regularly reinforced
- 'pitfalls' and 'examination tips' help you avoid commonly made mistakes and help you focus on what is required to perform well in your examination
- 'Test your understanding' activities are included within each chapter to apply your learning and develop your understanding.

ICONS

The chapters include the following icons throughout.

They are designed to assist you in your studies by identifying key definitions and the points at which you can test yourself on the knowledge gained.

Definition

These sections explain important areas of Knowledge which must be understood and reproduced in an assessment.

Example

The illustrative examples can be used to help develop an understanding of topics before attempting the activity exercises.

Test your understanding

These are exercises which give the opportunity to assess your understanding of all the assessment areas.

Quality and accuracy are of the utmost importance to us so if you spot an error in any of our products, please send an email to mykaplanreporting@kaplan.com with full details.

Our Quality Co-ordinator will work with our technical team to verify the error and take action to ensure it is corrected in future editions.

Progression

There are two elements of progression that we can measure: first how quickly students move through individual topics within a subject; and second how quickly they move from one course to the next. We know that there is an optimum for both, but it can vary from subject to subject and from student to student. However, using data and our experience of student performance over many years, we can make some generalisations.

A fixed period of study set out at the start of a course with key milestones is important. This can be within a subject, for example 'I will finish this topic by 30 June', or for overall achievement, such as 'I want to be qualified by the end of next year'.

Your qualification is cumulative, as earlier papers provide a foundation for your subsequent studies, so do not allow there to be too big a gap between one subject and another.

We know that exams encourage techniques that lead to some degree of short term retention, the result being that you will simply forget much of what you have already learned unless it is refreshed (look up Ebbinghaus Forgetting Curve for more details on this). This makes it more difficult as you move from one subject to another: not only will you have to learn the new subject, you will also have to relearn all the underpinning knowledge as well. This is very inefficient and slows down your overall progression which makes it more likely you may not succeed at all.

In addition, delaying your studies slows your path to qualification which can have negative impacts on your career, postponing the opportunity to apply for higher level positions and therefore higher pay.

You can use the following diagram showing the whole structure of your qualification to help you keep track of your progress.

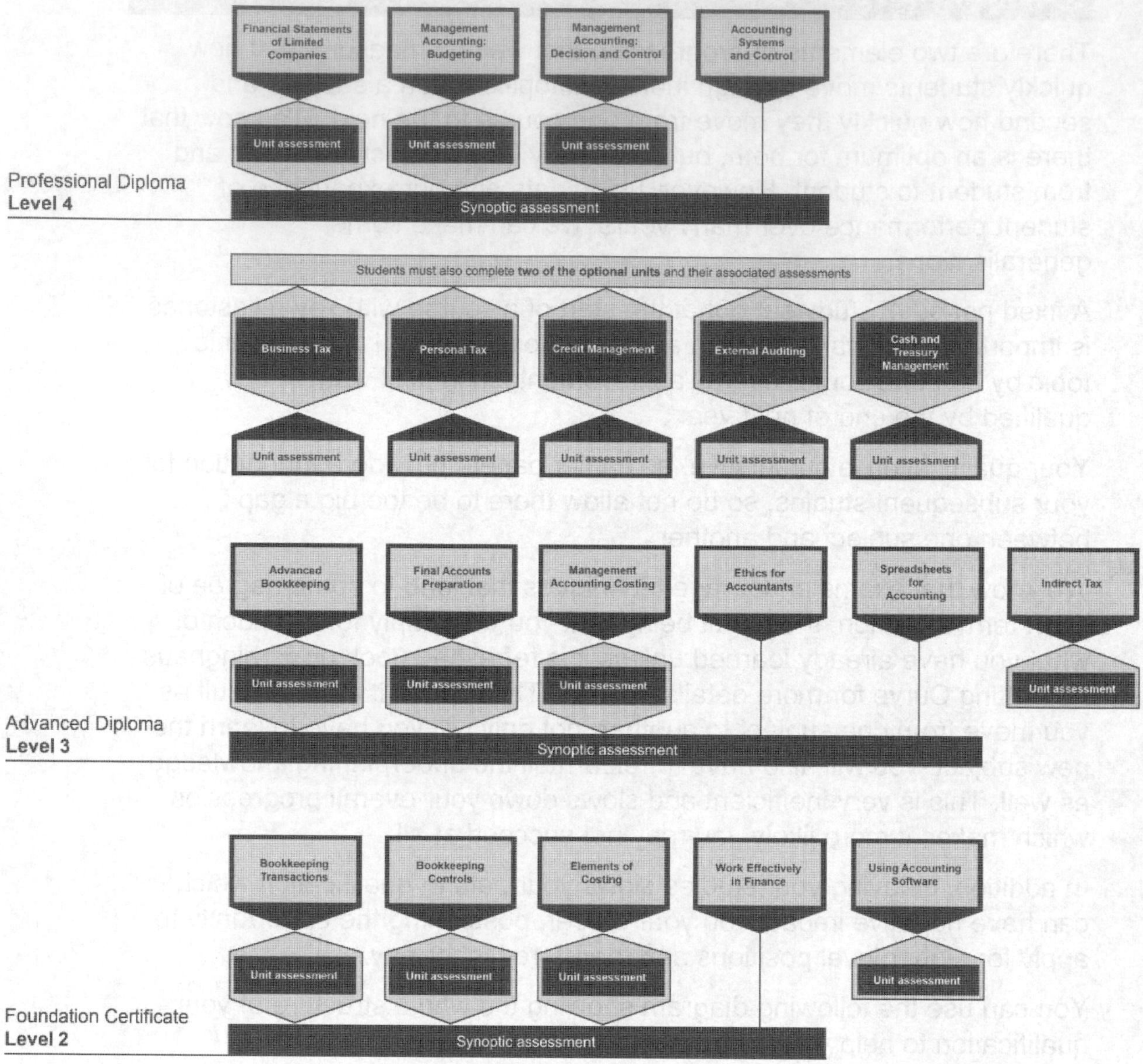
Financial Statements of Limited Companies
Management Accounting: Budgeting
Management Accounting: Decision and Control
Accounting Systems and Control
Unit assessment
Unit assessment
Unit assessment
Professional Diploma
Level 4
Synoptic assessment
Students must also complete two of the optional units and their associated assessments
Business Tax
Personal Tax
Credit Management
External Auditing
Cash and Treasury Management
Unit assessment
Unit assessment
Unit assessment
Unit assessment
Unit assessment
Advanced Bookkeeping
Final Accounts Preparation
Management Accounting Costing
Ethics for Accountants
Spreadsheets for Accounting
Indirect Tax
Unit assessment
Unit assessment
Unit assessment
Unit assessment
Advanced Diploma
Level 3
Synoptic assessment
Bookkeeping Transactions
Bookkeeping Controls
Elements of Costing
Work Effectively in Finance
Using Accounting Software
Unit assessment
Unit assessment
Unit assessment
Unit assessment
Foundation Certificate
Level 2
Synoptic assessment

UNIT GUIDE

Introduction

The purpose of this unit is to give students a basic introduction to costing, building a sound foundation in the knowledge and skills they need for more complex costing and management accounting units such as Level 3 Management Accounting: Costing and later, Level 4 Management Accounting: Budgeting.

Students will understand the importance of the costing system as a source of information for internal management decision-making. In contrast to the more outward perspective of financial accounting, the skills developed in this unit will allow students to provide information to managers that can be used to assist in internal business planning, decision making and control.

A student successfully completing this unit will be an effective member of the costing function within the accounting team. Working with the management/financial accountant and with supervision, they can be expected to:

- use the costing system to record and extract data and information for management purposes
- extract, compare and provide information on actual performance against budget.

This unit covers the nature of cost and how it is used in a costing system. Students will understand the different classifications of cost and how they can be used for internal management decision making. As well as classifying costs, students will code transactions and build up a unit cost for a product or service, using a range of techniques to cost material, labour and overheads. Students will also engage with the budgetary control system by comparing actual costs with budgeted costs and they will determine variances, noting whether they are adverse or favourable.

Essential to the unit is cost behaviour. Students will understand how cost behaves at different levels of output, and how variable and fixed costs per unit behave as output changes. The High-Low method, in its simplest format, is introduced to give students the underpinning knowledge and skill development for later units for management accounting at Levels 3 and 4, where marginal costing is used as an aid to management decision making.

Another important knowledge and skill that students will develop is to understand overhead as a component of cost and build a basic unit product cost using labour hours, machine hours and per unit as a basis. This will prepare students and give them the basic tools for studies in overhead apportionment, reapportionment and absorption at Level 3.

Elements of Costing is a **mandatory** unit in this qualification.

Learning outcomes

On completion of this unit the learner will be able to:

- understand the cost recording system within an organisation
- use cost recording techniques
- provide information on actual and budgeted costs and income

Scope of content

To perform this unit effectively you will need to know and understand the following:

		Chapter
1	**Understand the cost recording system within an organisation**	
1.1	**Recognise how costs are collected and classified in different types of organisation**	
	Students need to know:	
	• how costs are collected in different organisations	Throughout
	• what constitutes cost in different organisations and different types of organisation	
	• how elements of cost are classified: labour, material and overhead	1 2, 3
	• how costs are classified by nature: direct, indirect	
	• how costs are classified by behaviour: fixed, variable, semi-variable.	
1.2	**Recognise common costing techniques used in an organisation**	
	Students need to know:	
	• how product cost is determined: material, labour and overhead	3
	• inventory valuation methods: first-in-first-out (FIFO), last-in-first-out (LIFO), weighted average cost (AVCO)	3
	• labour costing methods: time-rate, overtime, piecework, bonus payments	4
	• overhead absorption methods: per unit, labour hours, machine hours.	3

		Chapter
1.3	**Identify the relationship between the costing and financial accounting systems within an organisation**	
	Students need to know:	
	• costing and financial accounting systems within an organisation	1
	• how each system uses cost: costing using many classifications of cost, financial accounting depending on historic cost.	
1.4	**Identify sources of information about income and expenditure**	
	Students need to know:	
	• how historic cost is used for accounting and costing reporting	1
	• how costing systems use actual or budgeted costs to determine unit/job cost	5
	• how budgeted and actual costs are used for planning and control purposes.	
1.5	**Distinguish between cost, profit and investment centres**	
	Students need to know:	
	• differences between cost centres, profit centres and investment centres	1
	• how each system uses cost: costing using many classifications of cost, financial accounting depending on historic cost.	
1.6	**Identify how materials, labour and overheads are classified and recorded**	
	Students need to know:	
	• how costs are classified: element, nature, behaviour, function	1
	• how costs are coded using numeric, alphabetic and alphanumeric coding systems	2
	• the components and construction of a manufacturing account.	3

		Chapter
2	**Use cost recording techniques**	
2.1	**Calculate cost of inventory issues and inventory valuations** Students need to be able to: • cost issue of inventory for management accounting purposes using FIFO, LIFO and AVCO • calculate closing values of inventory using FIFO, LIFO and AVCO (rounding figures as necessary).	3
2.2	**Calculate labour payments** Students need to be able to: • calculate labour payments: time-rate and overtime, piecework, bonuses.	4
2.3	**Calculate overhead absorption rates** Students need to be able to: • calculate simple overhead absorption rates: per unit, labour hours, machine hours (rounding figures as necessary) to show differing methods to arrive at unit cost.	3
2.4	**Use cost behaviour to calculate total and unit costs** Students need to be able to: • calculate total and unit costs at different levels of output • apply simple High-Low method to arrive at output costs at differing levels of output.	1

		Chapter
2.5	**Calculate the direct cost of a product** Students need to know: • how direct cost is a component of product cost	1
	Students need to be able to: • calculate direct cost of a product in a manufacturing organisation taking into account the flow of inventory in the production process, what constitutes direct cost, manufacturing cost, cost of goods manufactured and cost of goods sold.	3
3	**Provide information on actual and budgeted costs and income**	
3.1	**Compare actual and budgeted costs and income** Students need to be able to: • calculate differences between actual and budgeted costs and income • identify whether variance is adverse or favourable for costs and income.	5
3.2	**Apply exception reporting to identify significant variances** Students need to be able to: • calculate variances as a percentage of budget • identify significant variances according to an organisation's policy • report significant variances to a relevant manager.	5

Delivering this unit

Unit name	Content links	Suggested order of delivery
Bookkeeping Transactions	The use of codes in this unit links with Bookkeeping Transactions.	Bookkeeping Transactions might be delivered before, at the same time, or after Elements of Costing.

THE ASSESSMENT

Test specifications for this unit assessment

Assessment type	Marking type	Duration of exam
Computer based unit assessment	Computer marked	90 minutes

The assessment for this unit consists of 10 compulsory, independent, tasks.

The competency level for AAT assessment is 70%.

Learning outcomes		Weighting
1	Understand the cost recording system within an organisation	20%
2	Use cost recording techniques	60%
3	Provide information on actual and budgeted costs and income	20%
Total		100%

UNIT LINK TO SYNOPTIC ASSESSMENT

AAT AQ16 introduced a Synoptic Assessment, which students must complete if they are to achieve the appropriate qualification upon completion of a qualification. In the case of the Foundation Certificate in Accounting, students must pass all of the mandatory assessments and the Synoptic Assessment to achieve the qualification.

As a Synoptic Assessment is attempted following completion of individual units, it draws upon knowledge and understanding from those units. It may be appropriate for students to retain their study materials for individual units until they have successfully completed the Synoptic Assessment for that qualification.

With specific reference to this unit, the following learning objectives are also relevant to the Foundation Certificate in Accounting Synoptic Assessment

LO2 Use of cost recording techniques

LO3 Provide information on actual and budgeted costs and income

STUDY SKILLS

Preparing to study

Devise a study plan

Determine which times of the week you will study.

Split these times into sessions of at least one hour for study of new material. Any shorter periods could be used for revision or practice.

Put the times you plan to study onto a study plan for the weeks from now until the assessment and set yourself targets for each period of study – in your sessions make sure you cover the whole course, activities and the associated Test your understanding activities.

If you are studying more than one unit at a time, try to vary your subjects as this can help to keep you interested and see subjects as part of wider knowledge.

When working through your course, compare your progress with your plan and, if necessary, re-plan your work (perhaps including extra sessions) or, if you are ahead, do some extra revision/practice questions.

Effective studying

Active reading

You are not expected to learn the text by rote, rather, you must understand what you are reading and be able to use it to pass the assessment and develop good practice.

A good technique is to use SQ3Rs – Survey, Question, Read, Recall, Review:

1 **Survey the chapter**

Look at the headings and read the introduction, knowledge, skills and content, so as to get an overview of what the chapter deals with.

2 **Question**

Whilst undertaking the survey ask yourself the questions you hope the chapter will answer for you.

3 Read

Read through the chapter thoroughly working through the activities and, at the end, making sure that you can meet the learning objectives highlighted on the first page.

4 Recall

At the end of each section and at the end of the chapter, try to recall the main ideas of the section/chapter without referring to the text. This is best done after short break of a couple of minutes after the reading stage.

5 Review

Check that your recall notes are correct.

You may also find it helpful to re-read the chapter to try and see the topic(s) it deals with as a whole.

Note taking

Taking notes is a useful way of learning, but do not simply copy out the text.

The notes must:

- be in your own words
- be concise
- cover the key points
- be well organised
- be modified as you study further chapters in this text or in related ones.

Trying to summarise a chapter without referring to the text can be a useful way of determining which areas you know and which you don't.

Three ways of taking notes:

1 Summarise the key points of a chapter

2 Make linear notes

A list of headings, subdivided with sub-headings, listing the key points.

If you use linear notes, you can use different colours to highlight key points and keep topic areas together.

Use plenty of space to make your notes easy to use.

3 **Try a diagrammatic form**

The most common of which is a mind map.

To make a mind map, put the main heading in the centre of the paper and put a circle around it.

Draw lines radiating from this to the main sub-headings which again have circles around them.

Continue the process from the sub-headings to sub-sub-headings.

Annotating the text

You may find it useful to underline or highlight key points in your study text – but do be selective.

You may also wish to make notes in the margins.

Revision phase

Kaplan has produced material specifically designed for your final examination preparation for this unit.

These include pocket revision notes and an exam kit that includes a bank of revision questions specifically in the style of the new syllabus.

Further guidance on how to approach the final stage of your studies is given in these materials.

Further reading

In addition to this text, you should also read the 'Accounting Technician' magazine every month to keep abreast of any guidance from the examiners.

Cost classification

1

Introduction

This chapter introduces the concepts of financial and management accounting, the terminology of cost, profit and investment centres and looks in detail at different ways of classifying costs. It then looks at how total costs can be classified in more detail to enable cost planning for the future.

ASSESSMENT CRITERIA

Recognise how costs are collected and classified in different types of organisation (1.1)

Identify the relationship between the costing and financial accounting systems within an organisation (1.3)

Distinguish between cost, profit and investment centres (1.5)

Identify how materials, labour and expenses are classified and recorded (1.6)

Calculate the direct cost of a product or service (2.5)

CONTENTS

1 Financial accounting and management accounting

1.1 Introduction

Most businesses, whether large or small, generate large numbers of different types of transaction. To make sense of those transactions, they need to be recorded, summarised and analysed. In all businesses, it is the accounts department that performs these tasks.

From the raw data of the business's transactions, accountants provide **information for a wide range of interested parties**. Each party requires, however, slightly different information, dependent upon their interest in the business.

1.2 Financial accounting

Financial accounting provides information to **external groups**, such as the owners of the business, potential investors and HM Revenue and Customs (who uses this information to check that the business is paying the correct amount of tax).

Financial accounting could be described in simple terms as **keeping score**. The financial accounts produced are a **historic record** of transactions and are presented in a standard format laid down in law. These normally include:

- A statement of financial position (also known as a balance sheet).
- A statement of profit or loss (also known as an 'income statement' or 'profit and loss account').

Such statements are normally only produced **once or twice a year**.

Financial accounting is not, however, the only type of accounting. The other main type is Management accounting.

1.3 Management accounting

Management accounting provides information for **internal users**, such as the managers of the business.

Management accounting compares **actual results with predicted results** and tries to use information to make further predictions about the future.

It also provides information which managers can use to make **decisions**.

Management accounts can be produced in any format that is useful to the business and tend to be produced frequently, for instance every month.

1.4 The aims of management accounting

The aim of management accounting is to assist management in the following areas of running a business.

- **Planning**

  For example, through the preparation of annual budgets. This is a key aspect of management accounting.

- **Co-ordinating**

  Planning enables all departments to be co-ordinated and to work together.

- **Controlling**

  The comparison of actual results with the budget helps to identify areas where operations are not running according to plan.

  Investigating the causes, and acting on the results of that investigation, helps to control the activities of the business.

- **Communicating**

  Preparing budgets that are distributed to department managers helps to communicate the aims of the business to those managers.

- **Motivating**

  Management accounts include targets. These should motivate managers (and staff) and improve their performance.

  If the target is too difficult, however, it is likely to demotivate and it is unlikely to be achieved.

1.5 Useful management information

For **management information** to be of use to a particular group of managers, it must have the following attributes:

- **Relevant to their responsibilities.** For example, a production manager will want information about inventories, production levels, production performance, etc. within his particular department.
- **Relevant to particular decisions.** For example, if deciding whether to close a division, managers would need to know the likely costs including lost sales, likely redundancies and so on.
- **Timely.** Information has to be up-to-date to be of any value.
- **Value.** The benefits of having the information must outweigh the cost of producing it.

1.6 Cost accounting

Cost accounting is part of management accounting. As its name suggests, it is concerned with **establishing costs**. It developed within manufacturing businesses where costs are most difficult to isolate and analyse.

Cost accounting is primarily directed at enabling management to perform the functions of **planning, control** and **decision making:**

(a) determining costs and profits during a control period

(b) valuing inventories of raw materials, work in progress and finished goods, and controlling inventory levels

(c) preparing budgets, forecasts and other control data for a forthcoming control period

(d) creating a reporting system which enables managers to take corrective action where necessary to control costs

(e) providing information for decision-making such as setting the selling price of products or services.

Items (a) and (b) are traditional **cost accounting roles**; (c) to (e) extend into management accounting.

Test your understanding 1

The table below lists some of the characteristics of financial accounting and management accounting systems.

Indicate the characteristics for each system by putting a tick in the relevant column of the table.

Characteristic	**Financial accounting**	**Management accounting**
Content can include anything useful.	☐	☐
To help managers run the business.	☐	☐
Formats dictated by accounting rules.	☐	☐
Looks mainly at historical information.	☐	☐
Produced for shareholders.	☐	☐

2 Terminology – cost units and cost centres

2.1 Cost units

To help with the above purposes of planning, control and decision making, businesses often need to calculate a cost per unit of output.

A key question, however, is what exactly we mean by a 'unit of output', or '**cost unit**'. This will mean different things to different businesses but we always looks at what the business produces.

- A car manufacturer will want to determine the cost of each car and probably different components as well.
- In a printing firm, the cost unit could be the specific customer order.
- For a paint manufacturer, the unit could be a litre of paint.
- An accountancy firm will want to know the costs incurred for each client. To help with this it is common to calculate the cost per hour of chargeable time spent by staff.
- A hospital might wish to calculate the cost per patient treated, the cost of providing a bed for each day or the cost of an operation.

2.2 Cost centres

A **cost centre** is a small part of a business for which costs are determined. This varies from business to business but could include any of the following:

- The Research and Development department
- The Human Resources function
- A warehouse
- A factory in a particular location.

It is important to recognise that cost centre costs are necessary for control purposes, as well as for relating costs to cost units. This is because the manager of a cost centre will be responsible for the costs incurred.

Test your understanding 2

Suggest **ONE** suitable cost unit and **TWO** cost centres for a college of Further Education.

2.3 Cost, profit and investment centres

Some businesses use the term 'cost centre' in a more precise way than that given above:

- A **cost centre** is when the manager of the centre (department or division or location or...) is responsible for costs but not revenue or investment. This is usually because the centre has no revenue stream.

  For example, a Research and Development department.

- A **profit centre** is when the manager of the centre (department or division or location or...) is responsible for costs and revenues but not investment.

  For example, a local supermarket where investment decisions are made by the main Board.

- An **investment centre** is when the manager of the centre (usually a division) is responsible for costs and revenues **and** the level of investment in the division.

  For example, the US subsidiary of a global firm. The CEO would usually have authority to open new factories, close others and so on.

3 Cost classification

3.1 Types of cost classification

Costs can be **classified** (collected into logical groups) in many ways. The particular classification selected will depend upon the purpose for which the resulting analysed data will be used, for example:

Purpose	**Classification**
Financial accounts	By function – cost of sales, distribution costs, administrative expenses.
Cost control	By element – materials, labour, other expenses.
Cost accounts	By relationship to cost units (by nature) – direct, indirect.
Budgeting, decision making	By behaviour – fixed, variable.

3.2 Cost classification by function

For financial accounting purposes costs are split into the following categories:

- **Cost of sales** – also known as production costs. This category could include production labour, materials, supervisor salaries and factory rent.
- **Distribution costs** – this includes selling and distribution costs such as sales team commission and delivery costs.
- **Administrative costs** – this includes head office costs, IT support, HR support and so on.
- **Finance** – this refers to money paid to providers of finance (for example banks) and includes bank charges and interest charged on loans.

Note that one cost you will meet in the exam is depreciation. This is a measure of how much an asset is wearing out or being used up. The classification will depend on which asset is being depreciated. For example:

- Cost of sales – depreciation on a machine in the production line.
- Distribution – depreciation of a delivery van.
- Admin – depreciation of a computer in the accounts department.

Test your understanding 3

James plc makes mobile phones. Classify the following costs by function in the table below.

Cost	Production	Admin	Distribution
Purchases of plastic to make phone cases.	☐	☐	☐
IT director's bonus.	☐	☐	☐
Depreciation of factory building.	☐	☐	☐
Salaries of production workers.	☐	☐	☐
Insurance of sales team laptops.	☐	☐	☐

3.3 Cost classification by element

The simplest classification you will meet in the exam is splitting costs according to element as follows:

- **Materials** – includes raw materials for a manufacturer or alternatively the cost of goods that are to be resold in a retail organisation.
- **Labour** – Labour costs can consist of not only basic pay but overtime, commissions and bonuses as well.
- **Overheads** – this may also be referred to as other expenses and includes electricity, depreciation, rent and so on.

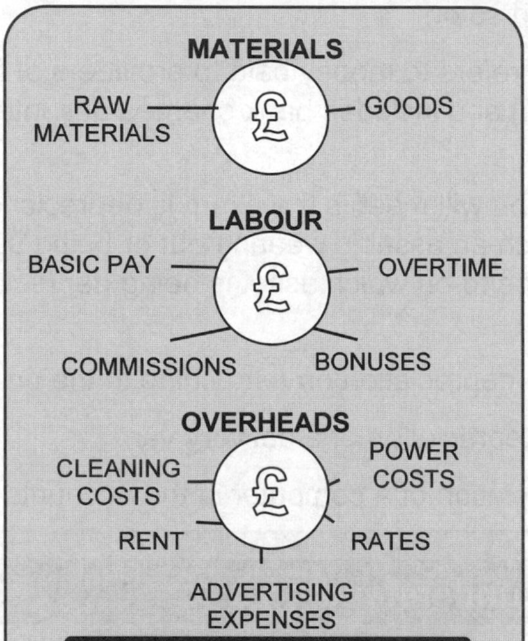

CLASSIFICATION OF COSTS

Test your understanding 4

Classify the following costs for a supermarket chain by element in the table below.

Cost	Materials	Labour	Overheads
Tins of baked beans.	☐	☐	☐
Lighting costs.	☐	☐	☐
Depreciation of freezers.	☐	☐	☐
Checkout staff salaries.	☐	☐	☐
Flour used in in-store bakery.	☐	☐	☐

3.4 Cost classification by nature – direct and indirect

To make calculating a cost per unit easier costs are split into the following categories:

- A direct cost is an item of cost that is traceable directly to a cost unit.

  For example, the cost of a bought-in engine for a car manufacturer.

  The total of all direct costs is known as the 'prime cost' per unit.

  An **indirect** cost is a cost that cannot easily be identified with any one finished unit. Such costs are often referred to as 'overheads'.

  For example, the rent on a factory.

You may notice that we have used the term 'overheads' in two different ways in the last two sections – once to refer to **expenses** (costs other than labour and materials) and once to refer to **indirect costs** (costs that can't be traced to individual units of production). In reality there are some direct costs that are not materials or labour, but they fall outside the range of this exam. This means that the term 'overhead' can be used to refer to indirect costs **or** expenses.

Test your understanding 5

Chadwicks runs a car repair service and garage. Classify the following costs by nature (direct or indirect) in the table below.

Cost	Direct	Indirect
Engine oil used in services.	☐	☐
Receptionist's wages.	☐	☐
Annual repairs to engine crane.	☐	☐
Brake pads.	☐	☐

Test your understanding 6

JJ Green is a furniture manufacturer. Classify the following costs by nature (direct or indirect) in the table below.

Cost	**Direct**	**Indirect**
Cost of wood and screws used.	☐	☐
Royalty payable as a result of using a particular chair design.	☐	☐
Oil used to lubricate the machines.	☐	☐
Salesmen's salaries.	☐	☐

3.5 Cost classification by behaviour – fixed and variable

For budgeting purposes, management needs to be able to predict **how costs will vary with differing levels of activity** (i.e. the number of cost units).

For example, if a furniture manufacturer expected to produce 1,000 chairs in a particular month, what should the budget be for the costs of wood, labour, oil, selling costs, factory heat and light, manager's salaries, etc.? How would these costs differ (if at all) if it expected to produce 2,000 chairs?

To make budgeting and forecasting easier, costs are split into the following categories:

- **Variable costs** are those that vary (usually assumed in direct proportion) with changes in level of activity.

  For example, if you make twice the number of chairs then the amount (and hence the cost) of wood used would double.

- **Fixed costs** are not affected by changes in activity level.

  For example, the rent on the factory.

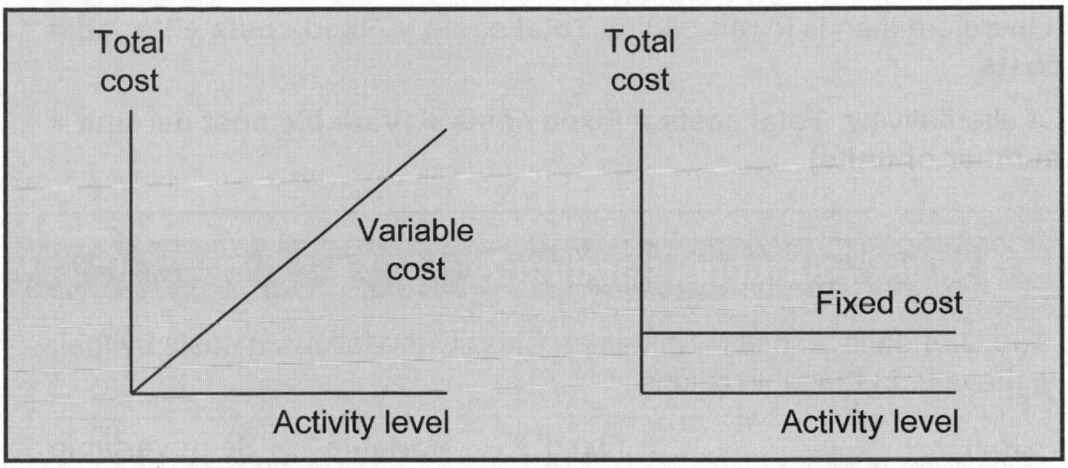

- **Semi-variable costs** are those that have a fixed element and a variable element.

  For example, the cost of electricity for the factory has a fixed element relating to lighting and a variable element relating to power used on the production line.

- **Stepped costs** are costs that remain fixed up to a particular level of activity, but which rise to a higher (fixed) level if activity goes beyond that range.

  For example, a firm may pay £40,000 per year to rent a factory in which they can produce up to 1 million units of product per year. However, if demand increases to more than 1 million units a second factory may be required, in which case the cost of factory rent may step up to, say, £80,000 per year and then be constant until we want to make 3 million.

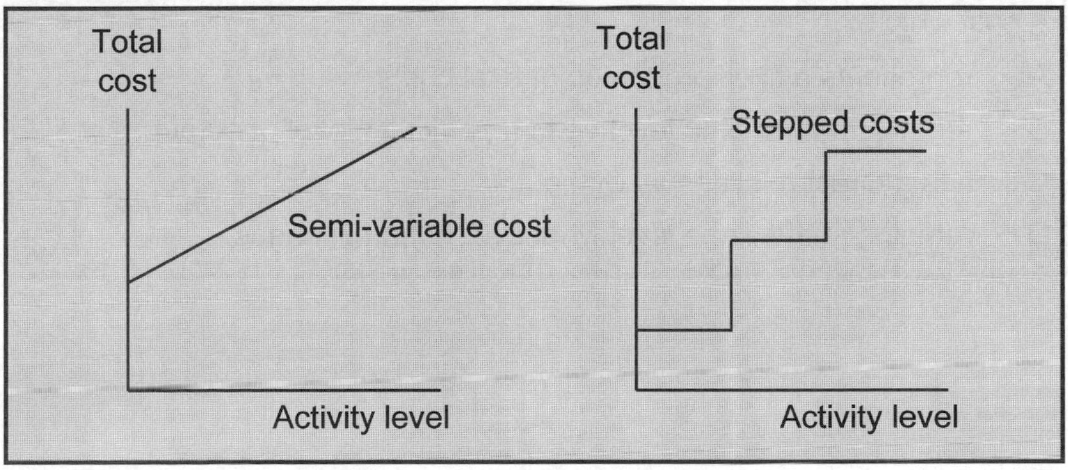

It therefore stands to reason that **Total costs = Fixed costs + Variable costs**

Or alternatively, **Total costs = Fixed costs + (Variable cost per unit × number of units)**.

Test your understanding 7

The Grande is a hotel in Sri Lanka. Classify the following costs by their behaviour in the table below.

Cost	**Fixed**	**Variable**	**Semi-variable**
Manager's salary.	☐	☐	☐
Cleaning materials.	☐	☐	☐
Food served in the restaurant.	☐	☐	☐
Electricity – includes a standing charge.	☐	☐	☐
Cleaner's wages (paid per room cleaned).	☐	☐	☐

Test your understanding 8

Which of the following best describes a 'pure' fixed cost?

A cost which:

A represents a fixed proportion of total costs

B remains at the same level up to a particular level of output

C has a direct relationship with output

D remains at the same level whenever output changes

Test your understanding 9

Identify the following statements as either true or false in the table below.

	True	False
Semi-variable costs have a fixed and variable element.	☐	☐
Fixed costs change directly with changes in activity.	☐	☐
Variable costs change directly with changes in activity.	☐	☐

3.6 Combining cost classifications

In some tasks in your assessment you may have to use more than one classification at a time. For example

- Factory rent is a production cost that is fixed (or stepped) and indirect.
- Direct materials are a production cost that is also variable.
- Direct labour is not necessarily a variable cost. For a car repair service, for example, it is possible to identify how much time a particular repair takes (by using job cards to record time) but the mechanic may be on a fixed salary per month.
- Sales commission is a variable selling and distribution cost.

Test your understanding 10

Identify the following statements as either true or false in the table below.

	True	False
All direct costs are variable.	☐	☐
All overheads are fixed.	☐	☐
Depreciation is always classified as an administrative cost.	☐	☐
All selling costs are fixed.	☐	☐

3.7 Why do organisations need to classify costs in different ways?

As you have seen in the previous sections, costs can be classified by nature, element, behaviour, or by function. Why do organisations need these different classifications?

The answer is that the different classifications will be used by the organisation for different purposes.

- **Classifying costs by element or nature** (materials, labour or overheads/direct and indirect costs) will be particularly useful for management accountants to help the business calculate how much each unit of product has cost to make. This can help the business decide how much to sell the product for.
- **Classifying costs by behaviour** (fixed, variable, stepped or semi-variable) will also be of use to management accountants, especially for the purpose of budgeting what the business' costs will be in future periods. For instance, if the business expects to double the number of units it makes next year, it will know that this will not affect the level of fixed costs, but would expect to double variable costs.
- **Classifying costs by function** (production, selling and distribution or administration) is of particular use to financial accountants, as it will help them to see the overall level of expenditure in each part of the organisation and therefore calculate total profit levels. This will then form part of the organisation's year-end financial accounts – in particular the income statement.

4 The high-low method

4.1 High-low method

If a semi-variable cost is incurred, it is often necessary to estimate the fixed element and the variable element of the cost for the purposes of budgeting.

Alternatively, if a question only gives information about **total** costs, without breaking that amount down into fixed and variable elements, it can be difficult to identify what costs will be for other levels of output.

Both of the above can be done by using the high-low method.

Remember:

Total cost = Fixed cost + (Variable cost per unit × number of units)

Example 1

A factory has incurred the following power costs in the last three months with different levels of production in each month:

	Production units	Power costs £
February	16,000	16,500
March	18,000	17,500
April	24,000	20,500

What are the fixed and variable elements of the power cost?

You should follow 3 basic steps to answer this problem:

Step 1

Find the highest and lowest levels of production (activity) and their related costs.

		Units	Cost £
High	April	24,000	20,500
Low	February	16,000	16,500

Step 2

Find the variable cost element by determining the increased power cost per unit between highest and lowest production levels.

		Units	Cost £
High	April	24,000	20,500
Low	February	16,000	16,500
	Difference	8,000	4,000

The power cost has increased by £4,000 for an increase in 8,000 units of production. The variable power cost is therefore:

$$\frac{£4,000}{8,000} = £0.50 \text{ per unit}$$

Step 3

Using either the highest or the lowest production level (from step 1) find the fixed cost element by deducting the total variable cost from the total cost.

		£
April	Total cost	20,500
	Total variable cost 24,000 × 0.5	(12,000)
		8,500

		£
February	Total cost	16,500
	Total variable cost 16,000 × 0.5	(8,000)
		8,500

You can then use this information to calculate costs for any other levels of output or activity, as seen below:

If production levels of 30,000 units are anticipated next month, what is the expected power cost?

The semi-variable power cost consists of the fixed cost (£8,500) and a variable cost per unit (£0.50). Therefore for an activity level of 30,000 units the total cost is predicted to be:

	£
Variable cost 30,000 × 0.50	15,000
Fixed cost	8,500
Total cost	23,500

Test your understanding 11

The electricity used in a factory has a semi-variable cost behaviour. The manager wants to know how much electricity to budget for if they were to make 75 units.

Units	Total cost
	£
10	120
50	200
100	300

A £150

B £100

C £250

D £137.50

5 Summary

In this introductory chapter we looked at some of the basic principles and terminology used in cost and management accounting. Costs can be classified in a variety of different ways for different purposes.

The basic classification is into materials, labour and expenses, each of which will be dealt with in detail in the following chapters.

A further method of classification of costs is between direct and indirect costs. You need to be aware of the difference between cost units (individual units of a product or service for which costs can be separately ascertained) and cost centres (locations or functions in respect of which costs are accumulated).

For decision-making and budgeting purposes, it is often useful to distinguish costs according to their behaviour as production levels change. The basic classifications according to behaviour are fixed and variable costs although there are also stepped costs and semi-variable costs.

The High-Low method can be used to identify fixed costs and variable costs when total costs are given for different levels of output.

6 Further Test your understanding exercises

Test your understanding 12

The table below lists some of the characteristics of financial accounting and management accounting systems. Indicate the characteristics for each system by putting a tick in the relevant column of the table.

Characteristic	**Financial accounting**	**Management accounting**
Content can include forecasts.	☐	☐
Looks mainly at historical information.	☐	☐
Format must conform to statute and accounting standards.	☐	☐
Any format can be used.	☐	☐
Mainly produced to help managers run and control the business.	☐	☐
Would be used by potential investors thinking of buying shares.	☐	☐
Produced for shareholders.	☐	☐

Test your understanding 13

Zenawi plc makes garden furniture.

Classify the following costs by function in the table below.

Cost	Production	Admin	Distribution
Purchases of wood to make chairs.	☐	☐	☐
Depreciation of delivery vans.	☐	☐	☐
HR director's bonus.	☐	☐	☐
Salaries of production workers.	☐	☐	☐
Electricity bill for workshop.	☐	☐	☐
Insurance of sales team laptops.	☐	☐	☐

Test your understanding 14

Kim and Yoshiro are the founding partners of an accountancy firm. They employ 20 accountants and have over 100 clients.

Classify the following costs by nature (direct or indirect) in the table below.

Cost	Direct	Indirect
Travelling costs for when staff visit clients.	☐	☐
Rechargeable accountants' time.	☐	☐
Office heating costs.	☐	☐
Recruitment costs.	☐	☐
Accountants' time recorded as 'general admin.' on time sheets.	☐	☐

Test your understanding 15

Elite Cars is a family-run business specialising in the sale, hire, servicing and repair of classic cars.

Classify the following costs by their behaviour in the table below.

Cost	Fixed	Variable	Semi-variable
Sales staff pay.	☐	☐	☐
Motor oil used in servicing.	☐	☐	☐
Depreciation of premises.	☐	☐	☐
Mechanics' pay (salaried).	☐	☐	☐
Electricity.	☐	☐	☐

Test your understanding 16

Jackson makes tables. His recent monthly production figures have been as follows:

Month	Units	Cost (£)
July	390	3,720
August	245	2,560
September	210	2,280
October	305	3,040

How much should he budget for in terms of costs for next month, given that he anticipates making 340 tables?

Test your understanding answers

Test your understanding 1

Characteristic	Financial accounting	Management accounting
Content can include anything useful.	☐	☑
To help managers run the business.	☐	☑
Formats dictated by accounting rules.	☑	☐
Looks mainly at historical information.	☑	☐
Produced for shareholders.	☑	☐

Test your understanding 2

Student hours = Cost unit

Computer room and library = Cost centres

Test your understanding 3

Cost	Production	Admin	Distribution
Purchases of plastic to make phone cases.	☑	☐	☐
IT director's bonus.	☐	☑	☐
Depreciation of factory building.	☑	☐	☐
Salaries of production workers.	☑	☐	☐
Insurance of sales team laptops.	☐	☐	☑

Test your understanding 4

Cost	Materials	Labour	Overheads
Tins of baked beans.	☑	☐	☐
Lighting costs.	☐	☐	☑
Depreciation of freezers.	☐	☐	☑
Checkout staff salaries.	☐	☑	☐
Flour used in in-store bakery.	☑	☐	☐

Test your understanding 5

Cost	Direct	Indirect
Engine oil used in services.	☑	☐
Receptionist's wages.	☐	☑
Annual repairs to engine crane.	☐	☑
Brake pads.	☑	☐

Test your understanding 6

Cost	Direct	Indirect
Cost of wood and screws used.	☑	☐
Royalty payable as a result of using a particular chair design.	☑	☐
Oil used to lubricate the machines.	☐	☑
Salesmen's salaries.	☐	☑

Note: You may have argued that oil was direct as you could calculate how much oil is needed per item made. However, it would be very difficult to determine the oil need for a **particular** item of furniture; hence the correct answer is indirect.

Test your understanding 7

Cost	Fixed	Variable	Semi-variable
Manager's salary.	☑	☐	☐
Cleaning materials.	☐	☑	☐
Food served in the restaurant.	☐	☑	☐
Electricity – includes a standing charge.	☐	☐	☑
Cleaner's wages (paid per room cleaned).	☐	☑	☐

Test your understanding 8

D – Pure fixed costs remain exactly the same in total regardless of the activity level.

Test your understanding 9

	True	False
Semi-variable costs have a fixed and variable element.	☑	☐
Fixed costs change directly with changes in activity.	☐	☑
Variable costs change directly with changes in activity.	☑	☐

Test your understanding 10

	True	False
All direct costs are variable.	☐	☑ Note 1
All overheads are fixed.	☐	☑ Note 2
Depreciation is always classified as an administrative cost.	☐	☑ Note 3
All selling costs are fixed.	☐	☑ Note 4

Note 1: Whereas direct materials are usually variable, direct labour may be fixed – e.g. lawyers may be on a fixed salary but produce detailed timesheets so a direct labour cost can be calculated for each client.

Note 2: Electricity is usually classified as an overhead but will have a variable element. If more units are made on a production line, then more electricity will be used (hence variable). However, it may not be possible or practical to measure exactly how much electricity is used to make a particular unit (hence indirect).

Note 3: For example, depreciation on production machinery would be included in cost of sales.

Note 4: Sales commission would be a variable selling cost.

Test your understanding 11

The answer is **C – £250**

Step 1

Find the highest and lowest levels of production and their costs:

	Units	£
High	100	300
Low	10	120
Difference	**90**	**180**

Step 2

Find the variable cost element by considering the differences:

Variable cost per unit = £180 ÷ 90 units = £2/unit

Step 3

Using either the highest or the lowest production level (from step 1) find the fixed cost element by deducting the total variable cost from the total cost.

For 100 units, fixed costs = £300 – (100 × £2) = £100

Therefore for 75 units total costs are £100 + (75 × £2) = £250

Test your understanding 12

Characteristic	Financial accounting	Management accounting
Content can include forecasts.	☐	☑
Looks mainly at historical information.	☑	☐
Format must conform to statute and accounting standards.	☑	☐
Any format can be used.	☐	☑
Mainly produced to help managers run and control the business.	☐	☑
Would be used by potential investors thinking of buying shares.	☑	☐
Produced for shareholders.	☑	☐

Test your understanding 13

Cost	Production	Admin	Distribution
Purchases of wood to make chairs.	☑	☐	☐
Depreciation of delivery vans.	☐	☐	☑
HR director's bonus.	☐	☑	☐
Salaries of production workers.	☑	☐	☐
Electricity bill for workshop.	☑	☐	☐
Insurance of sales team laptops.	☐	☐	☑

Test your understanding 14

Cost	Direct	Indirect
Travelling costs for when staff visit clients.	☑	☐
Rechargeable accountants' time.	☑	☐
Office heating costs.	☐	☑
Recruitment costs.	☐	☑
Accountants' time recorded as 'general admin.' on time sheets.	☐	☑

Test your understanding 15

Cost	Fixed	Variable	Semi-variable
Sales staff pay.	☐	☐	☑
Motor oil used in servicing.	☐	☑	☐
Depreciation of premises.	☑	☐	☐
Mechanics' pay (salaried).	☑	☐	☐
Electricity.	☐	☐	☑

Test your understanding 16

The highest output occurs in July, the lowest in September:

Month	Units	Cost (£)
July	390	3,720
September	210	2,280
Difference	180	1,440

The variable cost per unit is therefore £1,440 ÷ 180 units = £8

For July, fixed costs are £3,720 – (390 × £8) = £600

Therefore to produce 340 tables will cost £600 + (340 × £8) = **£3,320**

Coding of costs and income

2

Introduction

This chapter looks at the use of coding in organisations, including how income and expenditure is coded.

ASSESSMENT CRITERIA

Identify how materials, labour and overheads are classified and recorded (1.6)

CONTENTS

1 Classification and coding of costs

Cost accountants need to determine the costs that relate to each cost or profit centre. To make this simpler, each expense is classified according to its cost centre and type of expense.

A cost code is then allocated to the expense to represent this classification.

1.1 Coding systems

Definition

A **code** is a system of symbols designed to be applied to a classified set of items, to give a brief, accurate reference, which helps entry to the records, collation and analysis.

A cost code is a code used in a costing system.

1.2 Cost codes

In general, cost codes are constructed by deciding on the information that is needed. For most businesses we want to identify

(a) the profit or cost centre that is incurring the cost and

(b) the type of cost that is incurred.

There are no set methods of designing a cost code and the cost code of a particular organisation will be that which best suits the operations and costs of that business.

For example, if a business has only one division/operating centre, then there will be no need to identify that centre in the cost code. But if a business has several divisions, then the division that incurs the cost will need to be identified in the cost code.

Similarly, if the divisions have several cost centres and incur several different types of cost, then the cost code must be able to identify each of these.

There are a number of different methods of coding data:

- **numeric:** e.g. 100/310
- **alphabetic**: e.g. AB/RT
- **alpha-numeric**: e.g. A230

Example 1

Consider a company that has two operating divisions (North and South), two cost centres in each division (Construction and Despatch) with each cost centre incurring three types of cost (material, labour and expenses).

A typical cost code could be devised as follows

Step 1 Decide the structure of the cost code, for example **/**/**, where

First two digits	the operating division
Second two digits	the cost centre
Third two digits	the type of cost

Step 2 Allocate code numbers to the elements

(a) two operating divisions

North	01
South	02

(b) each division has two cost centres

Construction	01
Despatch	02

(c) each cost centre incurs three types of cost

Materials	01
Labour	02
Expense	03

Examples

Thus a cost code for expenses incurred by the despatch centre of the North division would be:

First two digits	the operating division	North	01
Second two digits	the cost centre	Despatch	02
Third two digits	the type of cost	Expenses	03

The cost code would therefore be: 01/02/03

Similarly, the code for materials purchased by the construction centre of the South would be 02/01/01.

1.3 More complex codes

Once a cost has been allocated its correct cost centre code then it may also be useful to know the particular type of expense involved. Therefore some more digits might be added to the cost centre code to represent the precise type of cost.

Example 2

If an expense for Machine Group 7 is for oil then its code might be 07 (for its cost centre) followed by 23 to represent materials followed by 04 to represent oil.

If an expense of the canteen is identified as frozen peas then its cost code might be 16 (its cost centre) followed by 02 to represent food purchases (materials) followed by 19 to represent frozen peas.

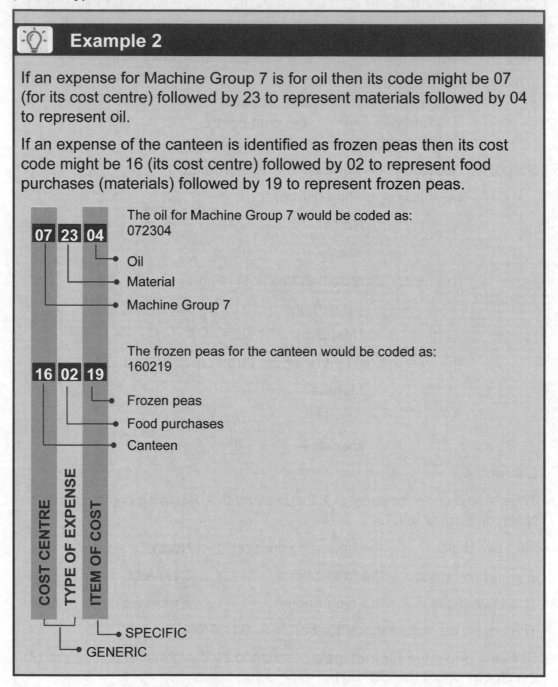

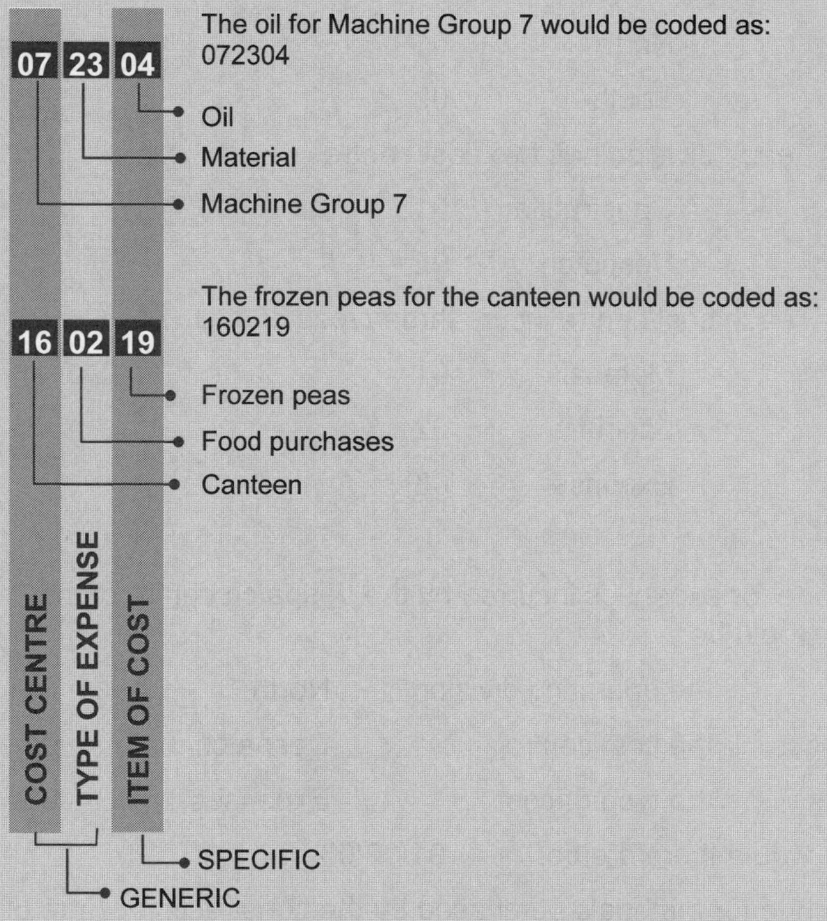

Test your understanding 1

Maxim Ltd, a manufacturer of garden lighting, uses a numerical coding structure based on one profit centre and three cost centres as outlined below. Each code has a sub-code so each transaction will be coded as ***/***.

Profit/cost centre	Code	Sub-classification	Sub-code
Sales	100	Sales to the public	100
		Sales to retailers	200
Production	200	Direct costs	100
		Indirect costs	200
Selling and distribution	300	Direct costs	100
		Indirect costs	200
Administration	400	Direct costs	100
		Indirect costs	200

Code the following revenue and expense transactions, which have been extracted from purchase invoices, sales invoices and payroll, using the table below.

Transaction	Code
Wages for staff working in the factory canteen.	
Sales to a French retailer.	
Sales to individuals via the company website.	
Depreciation on cars provided to salesmen.	
Bulbs for use in the garden lighting products.	
Chief accountant's salary.	

Test your understanding 2

Owen Ltd manufactures motorbike helmets.

It has two factories that are coded as:

Slough	S
Leeds	L

Each factory has the following cost centres:

Machining	120
Finishing	121
Packing	122
Stores	123
Canteen	124
Maintenance	125
Administration	126

Type of expense:

Labour	200
Material	201
Expenses	202

Sales revenue: 210

Thus, the cost of production labour in the Finishing Department at the Leeds factory would be coded L/121/200.

Code the following expenses using the table below.

Transaction	**Code**
Slough factory, cleaning materials used in the canteen.	
Slough factory, wages for stores personnel.	
Leeds factory, electricity for Machining Department.	
Leeds factory, telephone account for site as a whole.	
Slough factory, general maintenance material for repairs.	

Test your understanding 3

Jian plc manufactures computer printers and wishes to start coding its costs. It has decided to use an alphabetic code, based on the nature and the element of each cost, as well as the function it relates to.

The first part of the code will depend on whether the cost is direct or indirect.

Direct	J
Indirect	F

The second part of the code will depend on whether the cost is materials, labour or overheads (expenses).

Labour	HF
Materials	MB
Overheads	VV

The third part of the code will depend on the function that the cost relates to.

Production	PR
Administration	AD
Sales and distribution	SD

Thus, the cost of indirect production materials would be coded F/MB/PR

Code the following expenses using the table below.

Transaction	Code
Purchase of plastic used in the production of printers.	
Electricity used in Jian's administration head office.	
Wages paid to the cleaner of Jian's delivery vans.	
Purchase of ink for the head office printers.	
Salary paid to Jian's factory supervisor.	

1.4 Purpose of cost codes

The main purposes of cost codes are to:

- **assist precise information:** costs incurred can be associated with pre-established codes, so reducing variations in classification
- **facilitate electronic data processing:** computer analysis, summarisation and presentation of data can be performed more easily through the use of codes
- **facilitate a logical and systematic arrangement of costing records:** accounts can be arranged in blocks of codes permitting additional codes to be inserted in logical order
- **simplify comparison of totals of similar expenses** rather than all of the individual items
- **incorporate check codes** within the main code to check the accuracy of the postings.

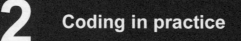

2 Coding in practice

2.1 Timing of coding

In order to be of most use the coding of costs should take place when the cost or expense is first received by the organisation. In most cases this will be when the invoice for the goods is received.

After this point the documents will be entered into the accounting system and then to the filing system so it is important that the coding is done immediately.

2.2 Receiving an invoice

When an invoice is received by the organisation it will undergo a variety of checks to ensure that it is for valid purchases that were ordered and have been received or that it is for a service that has been received.

In the process of these checks it will become clear what type of goods or service is being dealt with, for example it may be an invoice for the purchase of raw materials for the factory or an electricity bill for the entire organisation.

Once the invoice has been checked for validity then it must be correctly coded.

2.3 Choosing the correct code

In order for the correct code to be given to the invoice, it is vital that the person responsible for the coding fully understands the nature of the organisation and the costs that it incurs. The organisation's coding listing should be referred to and the correct cost centre, type and expense code should be entered on the front of the invoice.

2.4 Cheque and cash payments

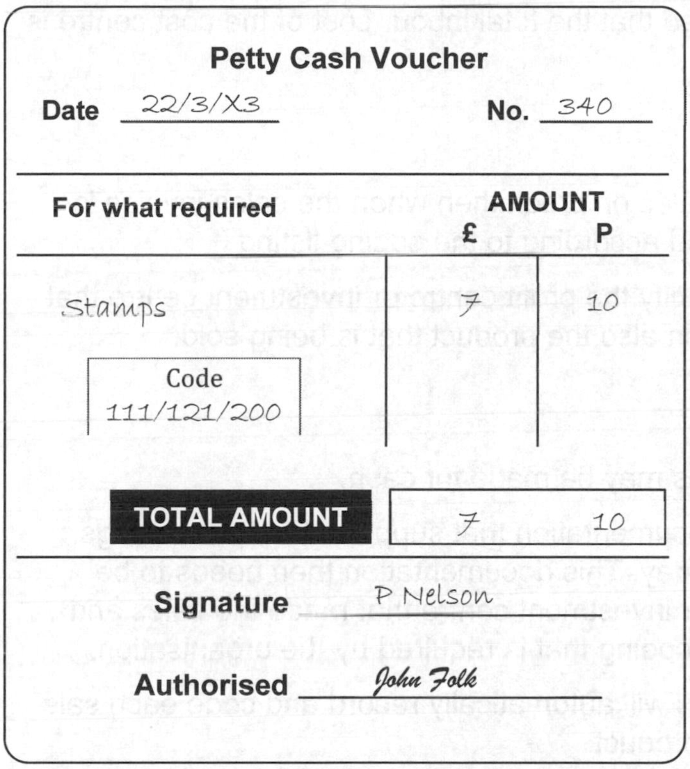
Petty Cash Voucher

Date 22/3/X3 No. 340

For what required	AMOUNT £	P
Stamps (Code 111/121/200)	7	10
TOTAL AMOUNT	7	10

Signature P Nelson

Authorised John Folk

As well as receiving invoices for costs incurred on credit most organisations will also write cheques for costs and even pay some costs out of petty cash. These costs must be coded in just the same way as purchases or expenses on credit.

If the payment is by cheque then there will be some documentation to support that payment. When this documentation is authorised for payment then it should also be coded for costing purposes.

If payments are made out of petty cash then they must be supported by a petty cash voucher. Again this voucher must be coded according to the type of cost.

2.5 Shared costs

Shared costs are costs that do not relate specifically to a particular cost centre. Some costs, for example electricity bills, cannot be allocated directly to a single cost centre as they are indirect costs which relate to a number of cost centres. Eventually a portion of this electricity bill will be shared out to each of the cost centres that use electricity but at the point where the account is being coded it must simply be recognised that this is a shared cost and not a cost that should be coded to a particular cost centre.

Therefore, the coding structure of the organisation should include some codes that specifically identify a cost as a shared cost.

2.6 Payment of wages and salaries

Wages and salaries normally form a very large part of the costs incurred by an organisation. If wages or salaries are paid by cheque or in cash then the supporting documentation, the payslip, should be coded as with other cash payments.

However, frequently wages and salaries will usually be paid directly into employee's bank accounts through the BACS system. Therefore it is important that the wages and salaries costs are coded according to the department or cost centre so that the total labour cost of the cost centre is known.

2.7 Sales invoices

If an organisation makes sales on credit then when the sales invoice is produced it should be coded according to the coding listing.

This code will probably specify the profit centre or investment centre that has made the sale and often also the product that is being sold.

2.8 Cash sales

In a retail organisation sales may be made for cash.

There should always be documentation that supports the cash takings, such as the till rolls for the day. This documentation then needs to be coded to reflect the profit or investment centre that made the sales and any other detailed product coding that is required by the organisation.

Most modern cash registers will automatically record and code each sale using the bar code on the product.

2.9 Assets and liabilities

We have concentrated so far on the costing of costs and revenue. However there are other items that also need to be coded, for example assets and liabilities.

The sort of assets that may occur in the exam are fixed assets (or 'non-current assets') purchased for the business and current assets (for example, debtors or 'receivables').

Example 3

Codebreaker Ltd manufactures the Enigma game machine.

The company has bought a production machine for £5,000.

The coding system is structured as:

- First two digits refer to the profit centre (the Enigma machine is profit centre 08).
- The additional code digits for fixed assets for production are 2600.

The code for the expenditure made by purchasing the machine is

£5,000 082600

This code would be the instruction to the accountant (or the computer) to post £5,000 to the appropriate fixed asset account.

3 Problems with coding

3.1 Which code?

The main problem when coding documents is deciding which cost centre and analysis code to use; the documents may not clearly show which cost centre incurred the costs or the type of cost it is.

If you are unable to code a document try:

- looking in the organisation's procedures manual
- referring the query document to your supervisor.

3.2 Apportionment

As mentioned above, if more than one cost centre has incurred the cost (for example, a heating bill for the whole building), the cost needs to be shared between all of the cost centres (or apportioned).

Although it may be easy to simply share the costs equally between the cost centres, some cost centres may be bigger than others and therefore use more electricity/heating etc – so should receive a greater percentage of the cost.

You will learn more about methods of cost apportionment in later units in your studies.

4 Summary

You should now know the importance of coding of costs and income. If actual costs and income are to be used for management purposes then it is vital that they are correctly classified and coded to ensure that they are allocated to the correct cost, profit or investment centre and according to the correct type of costs – material, labour or expense. Only then can any useful management information be obtained.

5 Further Test your understanding exercises

Test your understanding 4

A company manufactures shoes and slippers in half-sizes in the following size ranges:

- Men 6 to 9½
- Ladies 3 to 9
- Boys 1 to 5½
- Girls 1 to 5

The company uses a seven-digit code to identify its finished products, which, reading from left to right, is built up as follows:

Digit one indicates whether the products are men, ladies, boys or girls. The numbers used are

1 – men
2 – ladies
3 – boys
4 – girls

Digit two denotes type of footwear (3 is shoes; 6 is slippers)

Digit three denotes colour (5 is green; 6 is burgundy, 1 is brown)

Digit four denotes the material of the upper part of the product (leather is 4)

Digit five denotes the material of the sole (leather is 1)

Digits six and seven denote size.

Example

Code 1613275 represents a pair of Men's slippers, brown suede, rubber sole, size 7½.

Task: Set suitable code numbers to the following:

Product	**Code**
Boys' shoes, brown leather uppers, rubber soles, size 4.	
Ladies' slippers, green suede uppers, rubber soles, size 4½.	
Girls' shoes, burgundy leather uppers, leather soles, size 3½.	

Test your understanding 5

The expenses of an international organisation are coded with a seven digit code system as follows:

First and second digits	–	location
Third and fourth digits	–	function
Final three digits	–	type of expense

Extracts from within the costing system are as follows:

Location	**Code**
London	10
Dublin	11
Lagos	12
Nairobi	13
Kuala Lumpur	17
Hong Kong	18

Function	**Code**
Production	20
Marketing	21
Accounts	23
Administration	24

Type of expense	**Code**
Factory rent	201
Stationery	202
Telephone	203
Travel	204
Entertainment	205

Examples of the codes are as follows:

Factory rent in Nairobi:	1320201
Stationery purchased in London office:	1024202

Task:

Code the following revenue and expense transactions, which have been extracted from purchase invoices, sales invoices and payroll, using the table below.

Transaction	**Code**
Factory rent in the Dublin factory.	
Administration telephone costs incurred in Lagos.	
Salesman in Hong Kong entertaining an overseas visitor.	
Marketing brochures ordered in London.	

Test your understanding answers

Test your understanding 1

Transaction	Code
Wages for staff working in the factory canteen.	200/200
Sales to a French retailer.	100/200
Sales to individuals via the company website.	100/100
Depreciation on cars provided to salesmen.	300/200
Bulbs for use in the garden lighting products.	200/100
Chief accountant's salary.	400/200

Test your understanding 2

Transaction	Code
Slough factory, cleaning materials used in the canteen.	S/124/201
Slough factory, wages for stores personnel.	S/123/200
Leeds factory, electricity for Machining Department.	L/120/202
Leeds factory, telephone account for site as a whole.	L/126/202
Slough factory, general maintenance material for repairs.	S/125/201

Test your understanding 3

Transaction	Code
Purchase of plastic used in the production of printers.	J/MB/PR
Electricity used in Jian's administration head office.	F/VV/AD
Wages paid to the cleaner of Jian's delivery vans.	F/HF/SD
Purchase of ink for the head office printers.	F/MB/AD
Salary paid to Jian's factory supervisor.	F/HF/PR

Test your understanding 4

Product	Code
Boys' shoes, brown leather uppers, rubber soles, size 4.	3314240
Ladies slippers, green suede uppers, rubber soles, size 4½.	2653245
Girls' shoes, burgundy leather uppers, leather soles, size 3½.	4364135

(i) Boys shoes, brown leather uppers, rubber soles, size 4.

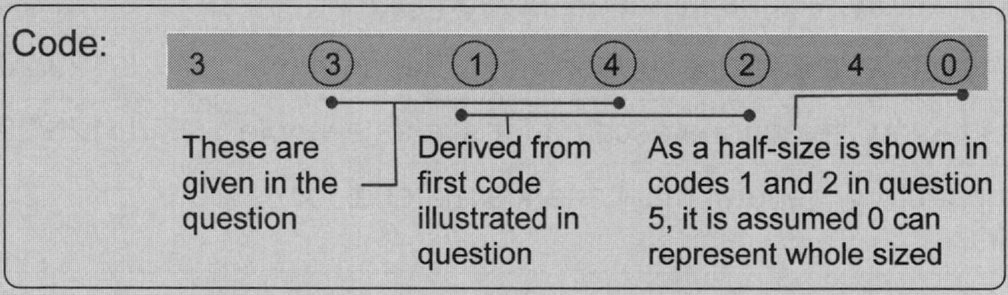
Code:
3 3 1 4 2 4 0
These are given in the question
Derived from first code illustrated in question
As a half-size is shown in codes 1 and 2 in question 5, it is assumed 0 can represent whole sized

(ii) Ladies slippers, green suede uppers, rubber soles, size 4½.

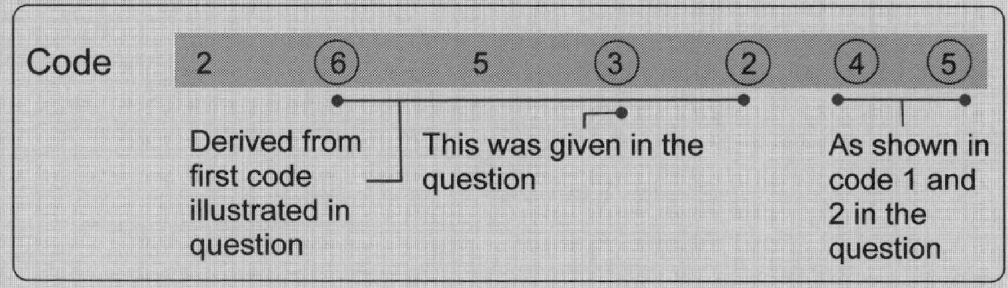
Code
2 6 5 3 2 4 5
Derived from first code illustrated in question
This was given in the question
As shown in code 1 and 2 in the question

(iii) Girls shoes, burgundy leather uppers, leather soles, size 3½.

Code 4 (3) 6 (4) (1) 3 5

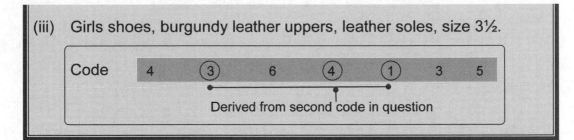

Derived from second code in question

Test your understanding 5

Transaction	Code
Factory rent in the Dublin factory.	1120201
Administration telephone costs incurred in Lagos.	1224203
Salesman in Hong Kong entertaining an overseas visitor.	1821205
Marketing brochures ordered in London.	1021202

Materials and inventory

3

Introduction

This chapter considers in more detail materials, the different types of inventory and how inventories are valued and classified.

ASSESSMENT CRITERIA
Recognise common costing techniques used in an organisation (1.2)
Calculate cost of inventory issues and inventory valuations (2.1)
Calculate the direct cost of a product (2.5)

CONTENTS

1 Different types of inventory

1.1 The production cycle

For a retailer the main type of inventory will be goods bought for resale.

For a manufacturer, however, we can identify three types of inventory:

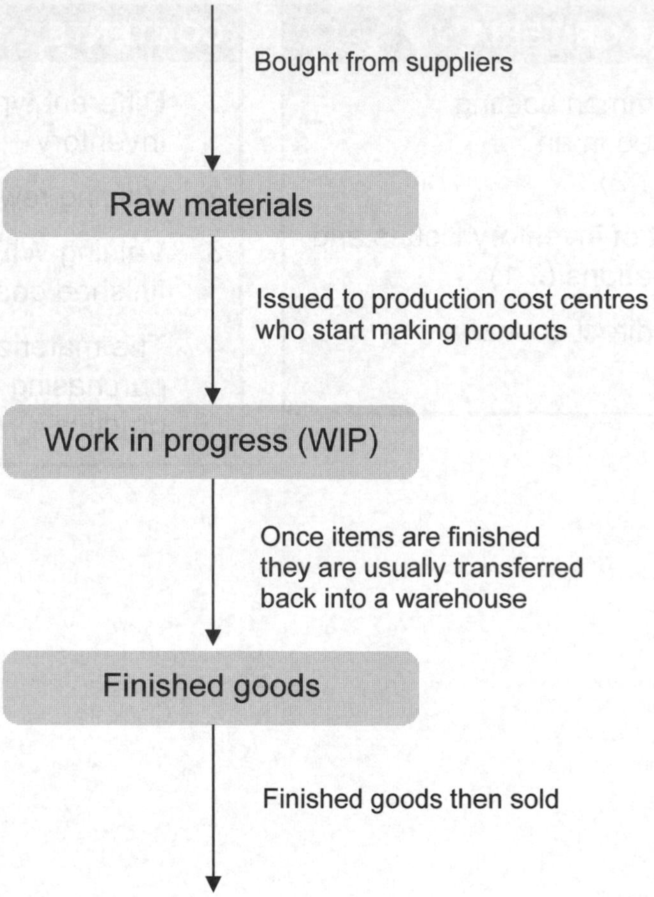

You may also see 'inventory' referred to as 'stock'.

1.2 Materials

For manufacturers various materials are needed to make the main product of the business.

Remember that, for management accounting purposes, costs can be classified as either direct or indirect. Materials are no exception to this.

Definition

Direct materials are the materials that are used directly as part of the production of the goods that the organisation makes.

The direct materials are therefore the raw materials that are part of the manufacturing process. In a business that makes wooden furniture the direct materials would for example include wood, hinges and polish.

Definition

Indirect materials are other materials used in the production process which are not used in the actual products themselves.

So for example lubricant for the machines that make the wooden furniture would be classified as indirect materials as it would be extremely difficult to identify how much lubricant was used to make a particular chair, say.

Definition

The total **direct** cost for a product (the direct materials and direct labour costs of producing it) is sometimes referred to as the **prime cost**.

1.3 Work in progress

Work in progress (WIP) refers to units that have been started but are incomplete at the end of the accounting period.

For example a wooden table may have had the top made but is still waiting for legs to be attached.

1.4 Finished goods

Finished goods are completed and ready for selling to customers.

2 Valuing raw materials

2.1 Introduction

There are two aspects to valuing raw materials:

- Firstly we need to determine the cost of materials issued to production cost centres.
- Secondly we need to be able to value the inventory of raw materials left in stores.

The cost of materials purchased will normally be derived from suppliers' invoices but, where many purchases have been made at differing prices, a decision has to be taken as to which cost is used when inventory is issued to the user department (cost centre).

Example 1

Petra Ltd has the following movements in a certain type of inventory into and out of it stores for the month of May:

Date	Receipts			Issues	
	Kg	Price/kg	Cost	Kg	Cost
May 1	200	£9.00	£1,800		
May 2	100	£10.80	£1,080		
May 3				50	?

What is the cost of materials issued on May 3?

Should we use £9/kg, £10.80/kg or something in between?

2.2 Methods of pricing issues of materials

Various methods exist including:

(a) FIFO (first in, first out)

(b) LIFO (last in, first out)

(c) Weighted average (AVCO)

The choice of method will not only affect the charge to the user department for which the material is required, but also the value of the inventory left in stores.

These systems attempt to reflect the movements of individual units in and out of inventory under different assumptions.

- **FIFO** – assumes that issues will be made from the oldest inventory available, leaving the latest purchases in inventory. This means that transfers from stores to production will be made at the oldest prices and the newest prices will be used to value the remaining inventory.

  FIFO is particularly useful when products are perishable and you want the oldest used first to avoid it going off or becoming out of date e.g. milk.

- **LIFO** – assumes that issues will be made from the newest inventory available, leaving the earliest purchases in inventory. This means that transfers from stores to production will be made at the newest prices and the older prices will be used to value the remaining inventory.

  LIFO could be used when products are not perishable e.g. stationery.

- **AVCO** – assumes that the issues into production will be made at an average price. This is calculated by taking the total value of the inventory and dividing it by the total units in inventory, thus finding the average price per unit. A new average cost is calculated before each issue to production.

  AVCO could be used when individual units of material are not separately definable e.g. sand at a builders merchants.

Example 1 – continued

Petra Ltd has the following movements in a certain type of inventory into and out of it stores for the month of May:

Date	**Receipts**			**Issues**	
	Kg	Price/kg	Cost	Kg	Cost
May 1	200	£9.00	£1,800		
May 2	100	£10.80	£1,080		
May 3				50	

Complete the table below for the issue and closing inventory values.

Method	**Cost of issue**	**Closing inventory**
FIFO		
LIFO		
AVCO		

Solution

Method	Cost of issue	Closing inventory
FIFO	£450	£2,430
LIFO	£540	£2,340
AVCO	£480	£2,400

Workings:

FIFO

- The 50 kg issued on May 3rd will all come from the **earliest** purchase made on May 1st
- Thus the cost of the issue will be 50 kg @ 9 = £450
- There are two ways to get closing inventory
- The first is to look at the flow of units : closing inventory will be 150 kg @ £9 (the remaining inventory from the May 1st purchase) and 100 kg @ £10.80 = £2,430
- The second approach, which will probably be easier in the exam, is to consider total purchases and simply deduct issues. Total purchases = £2,880, so closing inventory = 2,880 – 450 = £2,430

LIFO

- The 50 kg issued on May 3rd will all come from the **most recent** purchase made on May 2nd
- Thus the cost of the issue will be 50 kg @ £10.80 = £540
- Closing inventory = 2,880 – 540 = £2,340
- **OR** closing inventory will be 200 kg @ £9 (May 1st purchase) and 50 kg @ £10.80 (the remaining inventory from May 2nd) = £2,340

AVCO

- We bought 300 kg at a total cost of 200 @ £9 + 100 @ £10.80 = £2,880
- On average this works out at 2,880/300 = £9.60/kg
- Thus the cost of the issue will be 50 kg @ 9.60 = £480
- Closing inventory = 2,880 – 480 = £2,400
- **OR** closing inventory carried forwards will have the same average cost per unit so will be 250 kg @ £9.60 = £2,400

Test your understanding 1

Krully Ltd has the following movements in a certain type of inventory into and out of its stores for the month of June:

Date	Receipts		Issues	
	Units	Cost	Units	Cost
June 2	100	£400		
June 3	200	£1,000		
June 6	200	£1,200		
June 19			400	
June 25	400	£2,500		

Complete the table below for the issue and closing inventory values.

Method	Cost of issue on 19 June	Closing inventory at 30 June
FIFO		
LIFO		
AVCO		

Test your understanding 2

Jetty Ltd has opening inventory of raw material X of 1,500 units at £2 per unit. In the month another 1,000 units at £4.50 are received and the following week 1,800 units are issued.

Identify whether the statements in the table below are true or false by putting a tick in the relevant column.

Statement	True	False
FIFO values the closing inventory at £1,400.	☐	☐
LIFO costs the issue at £6,100.	☐	☐
AVCO costs the issue at £5,400.	☐	☐

2.3 Determining which method of inventory valuation has been used

You may be given a completed or partially completed inventory card and asked to decide which of the three methods have been used to produce it.

Example 2

JJJ Ltd has the following movements in a certain type of inventory into and out of it stores for the month of June:

Date	Receipts			Issues	
	Kg	Price/kg	Cost	Kg	Cost
June 1	500	£5.00	£2,500		
June 2	700	£6.00	£4,200		
June 3				900	£4,900

Identify the method JJJ has used to value its inventory and calculate the valuation of closing inventory using this method.

Solution

Method	Closing inventory
FIFO	£1,800

Workings:

The most reliable way of tackling this question is to look at the cost calculation that has been done for you – in this case the cost of the issue on June 3rd. If we calculate what this issue would be worth under each of the three valuation methods, we should be able to identify the approach that JJJ has taken.

LIFO

- The 900 kg issued on June 3rd will all come from the **most recent** purchases made.
- Thus the cost of the issue will be (700 kg @ £6) + (200 kg @ £5) = £5,200.
- As the cost of the issue is £4,900, the method being used is not LIFO.

AVCO

- We bought 1,200 kg at a total cost of (500 kg @ £5) + (700 kg @ £6) = £6,700
- On average this works out at £6,700/1,200 = £5.58/kg
- Thus the cost of the issue will be 900 kg @ £5.58/kg = £5,022

As the cost of the issue is £4,900, the method being used is not AVCO.

FIFO

- The 900 kg issued on June 3rd will all come from the **earliest** purchases.
- Thus the cost of the issue will be (500 kg @ £5) + (400 kg @ £6) = £4,900. As this is the value of the issue given, FIFO must be the valuation method used.
- Remember that there are two ways to get closing inventory.
- The first is to look at the flow of units: closing inventory will be 300 kg @ £6 (the remaining inventory from the June 2nd purchase).
- The second approach, which will probably be easier in the exam, is to consider total purchases and simply deduct issues. Total purchases = £6,700, so closing inventory = £6,700 – £4,900 = £1,800.

Test your understanding 3

Flotsam Ltd has opening inventory of raw material P of 3,000 units at £4.50 per unit. In the month another 2,000 units at £7 are received and the following week 3,750 units are issued.

Identify the valuation method described in the statements below by putting a tick in the relevant column.

Statement	FIFO	LIFO	AVCO
The closing inventory is valued at £6,875.	☐	☐	☐
The issue of 3,750 units is costed at £18,750.	☐	☐	☐
The issue of 3,750 units is costed at £21,875.	☐	☐	☐

2.4 Features of the different methods

FIFO is fairly easy to understand and has the following features:

- In times of rapidly increasing prices, material may be issued at an early and hence unrealistically low price, resulting in the particular job showing an unusually large profit.
- Two jobs started on the same day may show a different cost for the same quantity of the same material.
- In times of rapidly increasing prices FIFO will give a higher profit figure than LIFO or AVCO.

LIFO is also fairly simple to follow and has the following features:

- In contrast to FIFO closing inventories will now be shown at the earliest prices which means that in times of rapidly increasing or decreasing prices, the inventory figure bears little resemblance to the current cost of replacement.
- As with FIFO, two jobs started on the same day may show a different cost for the same quantity of the same material.
- The LIFO method uses the latest prices for issues to production and therefore the cost obtained is more likely to be in line with other costs and selling prices.
- In times of rapidly increasing prices LIFO will give a lower profit figure than FIFO and AVCO.

AVCO is a compromise on valuation of inventory and issues and the average price rarely reflects the actual purchase price of the material.

Test your understanding 4

Identify the correct inventory valuation method from the characteristic given by putting a tick in the relevant column of the table below.

Characteristic	FIFO	LIFO	AVCO
• Issues are valued at the most recent purchase cost.	☐	☐	☐
• Inventory is valued at the average of the cost of purchases.	☐	☐	☐
• Inventory is valued at the most recent purchase cost.	☐	☐	☐

Test your understanding 5

Identify the following statements as either true or false.

Statement	True	False
• FIFO costs issues of inventory at the most recent purchase price.	☐	☐
• AVCO costs issues of inventory at the oldest purchase price.	☐	☐
• LIFO costs issues of inventory at the oldest purchase price.	☐	☐
• FIFO values closing inventory at the most recent purchase price.	☐	☐
• LIFO values closing inventory at the most recent purchase price.	☐	☐
• AVCO values closing inventory at the latest purchase price.	☐	☐

2.5 Impact on profit

The method used to value inventory can have an effect on the profit that is reported by the organisation in any reporting period, as shown in the following example:

Example 3

Zahra starts a new business as a retailer at the beginning of January, and records the following movements of inventory during the first week of trading:

Date	Purchases			Sales	
	Units	Price/unit	Cost	Units	Price/unit
Jan 3	400	£18.00	£7,200		
Jan 5	200	£21.60	£4,320		
Jan 7				250	£40.00

There was no opening inventory at the start of the week as it is a new business.

The value of closing inventory at the end of the week, using the different valuation methods, is:

- FIFO – £7,020
- LIFO – £6,300
- AVCO – £6,720

(You can check these values for yourself!)

The gross profit shown for each of the three valuation methods is as follows:

	FIFO £	**LIFO** £	**AVCO** £
Sales	**10,000**	**10,000**	**10,000**
Cost of sales:			
Opening inventory	0	0	0
Purchases	11,520	11,520	11,520
Closing inventory	(7,020)	(6,300)	(6,720)
	———	———	———
	4,500	**5,220**	**4,800**
Gross profit	**5,500**	**4,780**	**5,200**

However, whilst each of the 3 gross profit figures above are different, this is only because of a timing difference. In the long term, the overall profit reported by the organisation will be the same.

To continue with the example, suppose that Zahra buys £7,000 of goods in the following week, and sells all of her inventory for £14,000 (so that, at the end of that week, she has no inventory remaining).

The gross profit shown for week 2 for each of the 3 valuation methods would be as follows:

	FIFO £	LIFO £	AVCO £
Sales	**14,000**	**14,000**	**14,000**
Cost of sales:			
Opening inventory	7,020	6,300	6,720
Purchases	7,000	7,000	7,000
Closing inventory	(0)	(0)	(0)
	———	———	———
	14,020	**13,300**	**13,720**
Gross profit	**(20)**	**700**	**280**

Whilst the profit shown in each individual week depends on the inventory valuation method adopted, the overall profit for the whole period is always the same, at £5,480.

3 Valuing WIP and finished goods

3.1 Basic principles

When valuing WIP or finished goods we need to incorporate all the different costs incurred to bring it to its present location and condition. To make this easier, direct costs are included first and then indirect costs or overheads added.

Identifying direct materials and labour should be straightforward, or the costs would not be classified as 'direct':

- Direct materials could be identified using job cards and information on stores requisitions.
- Direct labour can be identified using job cards and time sheets.

Because it is more difficult to identify overheads with units of output some system needs to be developed for either averaging overheads over units or absorbing them into units. This is particularly important when a company makes more than one product.

This is discussed in more detail in other units in your studies, but here you need to be aware of three approaches:

- **Unit basis** – each unit gets the same level of overhead.
- **Labour rate basis** – here overheads are absorbed as a rate per direct labour hour. This means that for every hour someone works on the unit an hour's worth of overhead is given to the unit as well.
- **Machine hour basis** – here overheads are absorbed as a rate per direct machine hour. This means that for every hour a machine is used to make a unit an hour's worth of overhead is given to the unit as well.

Example 4

The cost per unit for completed goods could show the following:

	Unit cost
	£
Direct labour cost (2 hours @£10/hour)	20
Direct material cost	3
Direct expenses	1
Prime cost	24
Production overheads (2 hours @ £4/hour)	8
Total cost per unit	32

Example 5

A job card showing the WIP on job number 217 might look like the following:

JOB NO 217

Materials requisitions	**Quantity**	£	**Total** (£)
0254 G 3578	100 kg	4,200	
0261 K 3512	50 kg	3,150	
			7,350
Wages – employees	**Hours**	£	
13343	80	656	
15651	30	300	
12965	40	360	
	150		1,316
Overheads	**Hours**	£	
Absorption rate £12	150	1,800	1,800
Total cost			10,466

3.2 Overheads using a cost per unit basis

In the exam you may be asked to calculate a unit cost at a specified production level. When doing this, be careful to distinguish between fixed and variable costs and do not confuse total costs and unit costs.

Example 6

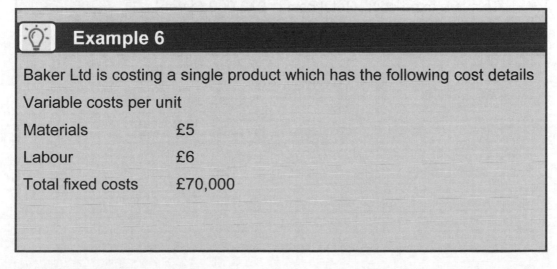

Baker Ltd is costing a single product which has the following cost details

Variable costs per unit

Materials	£5
Labour	£6
Total fixed costs	£70,000

Complete the following total cost and unit cost table for a production level of 20,000 units.

Element	Total cost	Unit cost
Materials	£	£
Labour	£	£
Overheads	£	£
Total	£	£

Solution

Element	Total cost	Unit cost
Materials	£100,000	£5.00
Labour	£120,000	£6.00
Overheads	£70,000	£3.50
Total	£290,000	£14.50

Workings:

Materials

- This is a variable cost – unit cost is £5 (given)
- Total cost will be 20,000 × £5 = £100,000

Labour

- This is a variable cost – unit cost is £6 (given)
- Total cost will be 20,000 × £6 = £120,000

Overheads

- This is a fixed cost – total cost is £70,000 (given)
- Unit cost will be 70,000 ÷ 20,000 = £3.50

Test your understanding 6

XYZ Ltd is costing a single product which has the following cost details

Variable costs per unit

Materials £4

Labour £5

Total fixed costs £60,000

Complete the following total cost and unit cost table for a production level of 15,000 units.

Element	Total cost	Unit cost
Materials	£	£
Labour	£	£
Overheads	£	£
Total	£	£

Example 7

Complete the table below showing fixed costs, variable costs, total costs and unit cost at the different levels of production.

Units	Fixed costs	Variable costs	Total costs	Unit cost
1,000	£20,000	£4,000	£24,000	£24.00
2,000	£	£	£	£
3,000	£	£	£	£
4,000	£	£	£	£

Solution

Units	Fixed costs	Variable costs	Total costs	Unit cost
1,000	£20,000	£4,000	£24,000	£24.00
2,000	£20,000	£8,000	£28,000	£14.00
3,000	£20,000	£12,000	£32,000	£10.67
4,000	£20,000	£16,000	£36,000	£9.00

Workings:

Fixed costs

- Unless there are stepped costs, the fixed costs will be the same at each activity level.

Variable costs – approach 1

- Calculate the variable cost per unit = £4,000/1,000 units = £4 per unit.
- This can then be used to get the total variable cost at different levels.

So for 3,000 units the total variable cost will be 3,000 × £4 = £12,000.

Variable costs – approach 2

- Alternatively you could scale up the total variable cost.
- For example, going from 1,000 to 3,000 units we have increased the number of units by a factor of 3 so need to do the same to the variable costs.
- This gives total variable cost = 3 × 4,000 = £12,000 as before.

Unit costs

- Simply divide the total cost by the number of units.
- E.g. for 4,000 units, unit costs = £36,000/4,000 = £9 per unit.

Test your understanding 7

Complete the table below showing fixed costs, variable costs, total costs and unit cost at the different levels of production.

Units	Fixed costs	Variable costs	Total costs	Unit cost
1,000	£60,000	£2,000	£62,000	£62.00
2,000	£	£	£	£
3,000	£	£	£	£
4,000	£	£	£	£

3.3 Overheads using a labour rate basis

The calculation is as before but rather than dividing by budgeted units, budgeted labour hours is used to find an overhead rate per labour hour. This would be useful in a business that is labour intensive.

Example 8

Martine Ltd is costing a single product which has the following cost details

Variable costs per unit

Materials	£4
Labour	£6
Total overheads	£40,000

Complete the following total cost and unit cost table for a production level of 10,000 units. Each unit takes 2 labour hours to make. Overheads are absorbed into units using a rate per labour hour basis.

Element	Total cost	Unit cost
Materials	£	£
Labour	£	£
Overheads	£	£
Total	£	£

Solution

Element	Total cost	Unit cost
Materials	£40,000	£4.00
Labour	£60,000	£6.00
Overheads	£40,000	£4.00
Total	£140,000	£14.00

Workings:

Materials

- This is a variable cost – unit cost is £4 (given)
- Total cost will be 10,000 × £4 = £40,000

Labour

- This is a variable cost – unit cost is £6 (given)
- Total cost will be 10,000 × £6 = £60,000

Overheads

- Total cost is £40,000 (given)
- Total labour hours = 10,000 units × 2 hours = 20,000 hours
- Overhead rate per labour hour = £40,000 ÷ 20,000 hours = £2.00
- Overhead cost per unit is therefore 2 hours × £2.00/hour = £4.00

Test your understanding 8

PQR Ltd is costing a single product which has the following cost details

Variable costs per unit

Materials	£6
Labour	£8
Total overheads	£90,000

Complete the following total cost and unit cost table for a production level of 15,000 units. Each unit takes 2 labour hours to make, and overheads are to be absorbed into units using a rate per labour hour.

Element	**Total cost**	**Unit cost**
Materials	£	£
Labour	£	£
Overheads	£	£
Total	£	£

3.4 Overheads using a machine hour rate basis

The calculation is as 3.3 above, but rather than calculating a labour rate per hour, budgeted machine hours is used to find an overhead rate per machine hour. This would be useful in a business that is machine intensive.

Example 9

Ahmed Ltd is costing one of the products it makes which has the following cost details:

Variable costs per unit

Materials	£5
Labour	£4
Total overheads	£60,000

Complete the following total cost and unit cost table for a production level of 20,000 units. Each unit takes 1.5 machine hours to make. Overheads are absorbed into units using a rate per machine hour basis.

Element	Total cost	Unit cost
Materials	£	£
Labour	£	£
Overheads	£	£
Total	£	£

Solution

Element	Total cost	Unit cost
Materials	£100,000	£5.00
Labour	£80,000	£4.00
Overheads	£60,000	£3.00
Total	£240,000	£12.00

Workings:

Materials

- This is a variable cost – unit cost is £5 (given)
- Total cost will be 20,000 × £5 = £100,000

Labour

- This is a variable cost – unit cost is £4 (given)
- Total cost will be 20,000 × £4 = £80,000

Overheads

- Total cost is £60,000 (given)
- Total machine hours = 20,000 units × 1.5 hours = 30,000 hours
- Overhead rate per machine hour = £60,000 ÷ 30,000 hours = £2.00
- Overhead cost per unit is therefore 1.5 hours × £2.00/hour = £3.00

Test your understanding 9

ABC Ltd is costing a product which has the following cost details:

Variable costs per unit

Materials	£3
Labour	£10
Total overheads	£120,000

Complete the following total cost and unit cost table for a production level of 12,000 units. Each unit takes 0.5 machine hours to make, and overheads are to be absorbed into units using a rate per machine hour.

Element	Total cost	Unit cost
Materials	£	£
Labour	£	£
Overheads	£	£
Total	£	£

3.5 Factory cost of goods sold

As well as valuing units for inventory purposes we also want to know the cost of goods sold. The main issue here is that we need to adjust the costs incurred within the period to take into account opening and closing inventory.

For a retailer:

Cost of sales = opening inventory + purchases – closing inventory

For a manufacturer there will be the further complication that there will be opening and closing inventories for raw materials, work in progress and finished goods. This could be shown as a full manufacturing account:

Example 10 – Manufacturing account

	£
Opening inventory of raw materials	7,000
Purchases of raw materials	50,000
Closing inventory of raw materials	(10,000)
DIRECT MATERIALS USED	47,000
Direct labour	97,000
DIRECT COST	**144,000**
Manufacturing overheads	53,000
MANUFACTURING COST	**197,000**
Opening inventory of work in progress	8,000
Closing inventory of work in progress	(10,000)
COST OF GOODS MANUFACTURED	**195,000**
Opening inventory of finished goods	30,000
Closing inventory of finished goods	(25,000)
COST OF GOODS SOLD	**200,000**

Test your understanding 10

Reorder the following costs into a manufacturing account format:

	£
Manufacturing overheads	47,000
Purchases of raw materials	60,000
MANUFACTURING COST	**147,000**
Opening inventory of raw materials	14,000
Closing inventory of finished goods	(70,000)
COST OF GOODS SOLD	**147,000**
DIRECT COST	**100,000**
Opening inventory of work in progress	42,000
DIRECT MATERIALS USED	64,000
Direct labour	36,000
Closing inventory of raw materials	(10,000)
Closing inventory of work in progress	(32,000)
COST OF GOODS MANUFACTURED	**157,000**
Opening inventory of finished goods	60,000

Test your understanding 11

A company has the following cost information for its last accounting period:

	£
Materials costs:	
Direct	50,000
Indirect	12,000
Labour costs:	
Direct	30,000
Indirect	6,000
Manufacturing expenses	82,000

Work in progress and finished goods inventories were as follows:

	£
Work in progress:	
Opening	7,000
Closing	5,000
Finished goods:	
Opening	15,000
Closing	0

Required:

Complete the table below to show the company's cost structure for the last accounting period:

	£
Prime cost	
Manufacturing overheads	
Total manufacturing costs	
Cost of goods manufactured	
Cost of goods sold	

4 The materials purchasing cycle in practice

4.1 Introduction

Materials can often form the largest single item of cost for a business so it is essential that the material purchased is the most suitable for the intended purpose.

4.2 Control of purchasing

When goods are purchased they must be ordered, received by the stores department, recorded, issued to the manufacturing department that requires them and eventually paid for. This process needs a great deal of paperwork and strict internal controls.

Internal control consists of full documentation and appropriate authorisation of all transactions, movements of materials and of all requisitions, orders, receipts and payments.

If control is to be maintained over purchasing, it is necessary to ensure that:

- only necessary items are purchased
- orders are placed with the most appropriate supplier after considering price and delivery details
- the goods that are actually received are the goods that were ordered and in the correct quantity
- the price paid for the goods is correct (i.e. what was agreed when the order was placed).

To ensure that all of this takes place requires a reliable system of checking and control.

4.3 Overview of procedures

It is useful to have an overview of the purchasing process.

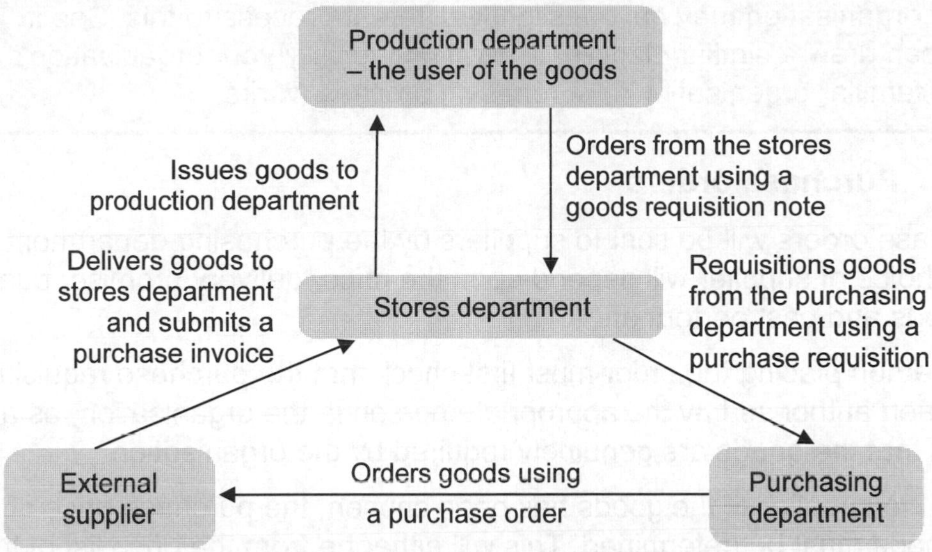

There are many variations of the above system in practice, but it is a fairly typical system and does provide good control over the purchasing and issuing process.

Test your understanding 12 (no feedback)

Your organisation may have a slightly different process to this. See if you can draw a similar diagram illustrating the way your organisation's (or a familiar organisation's) purchasing process works.

4.4 Purchase orders

Purchase orders will be sent to suppliers by the purchasing department. The choice of supplier will depend upon the price, delivery promise, quality of goods and past performance.

The person placing the order must first check that the purchase requisition has been authorised by the appropriate person in the organisation, as a check that the goods are genuinely required by the organisation.

Once the supplier of the goods has been chosen, the purchase price of the goods must be determined. This will either be from the price list of the supplier or from a special quotation of the price by that supplier. The price agreed will be entered on the purchase order together with details of the goods being ordered.

The purchase order must then be authorised by the appropriate person in the organisation before being dispatched to the supplier.

A copy of the purchase order is sent to the goods receiving department or stores department as confirmation of expected delivery. The goods receiving department therefore knows that goods are due and can alert appropriate management if they are not received. A copy is also sent to the accounts department to be matched to the supplier's invoice.
An example purchase order is shown overleaf.

Example 11

BLACKHILL FILES
742 St Anne's Way, York YO5 4NP
Telephone 01904 27635
Registered in England, No 1457893

PURCHASE ORDER

Printing Unlimited
80 New High Street
Exeter
EX4 2LP

Order No: 35762

Ref: T. Holmes

Date: 22 June 20X4

Please print 25,000 labels at £10.50 per 1,000.

Needed by 20 July 20X4.

Payment within 30 days of delivery.

2% early settlement discount.

Delivery to: As above

4.5 Purchase invoice

The supplier will submit a purchase invoice for goods detailing the amount that we must pay for them and the date that payment is due. The purchase invoice might be included when the goods themselves are delivered, or might be sent after delivery.

The purchase invoice is the primary source of information for recording the quantity and cost of materials purchased.

The person responsible for payment must check that the details of the purchase invoice agree to the purchase order.

This is to ensure that:

- what was ordered was received
- the price charged is that agreed.

Once it is certain that the purchase invoice agrees with the goods that were ordered then the invoice can be authorised for payment.

4.6 Bin cards

The storekeeper must know at any time how much of any item he has in inventory. This is done by use of a bin card.

> **Definition**
>
> A **bin card** is a simple record of receipts, issues and balances of inventory in hand kept by storekeepers, recorded in quantities of materials inventory.

The bin card is a duplication of the quantity information recorded in the stores ledger (see later in this chapter) but storekeepers frequently find that such a ready record is a very useful aid in carrying out their duties.

An example of a bin card for an item of inventory is given below.

BIN CARD

Description: Chipboard   Location: Stores   Code: D35

Maximum: 3,000m   Minimum: 1,000m   Reorder level: 1,400m   Reorder quantity: 200m

	Receipts			*Issues*				*On order*	
Date	GRN ref	Quantity	Issue date	Ref	Quantity	*Current inventory level*	Date	Ref	Quantity
04/7/X3	8737	200m				200m	01/8/X3	PO6752	300m
30/7/X3	8748	300m				500m			
			07/8/X3	3771	400m	100m			

The bin card does not have value columns.

4.7 Stores ledger account

As well as the information recorded by the storekeeper on a bin card, the accounts department also keeps records for each line of inventory, in terms of both quantity and value, and this is known as the stores ledger account.

> **Definition**
>
> A stores ledger account records the quantity and value of receipts and issues and the current balance of each item of inventory.

The stores ledger account for the item of inventory recorded in the bin card earlier in this section is given below:

STORES LEDGER ACCOUNT

Material Chipboard

Code D35

Date	Receipts				Issues				Balance		
	GRN Ref	Qty	Price per unit £	Amount £	Issue ref	Qty per unit	Price £	Amount	Qty per unit	Price £	Value £
30/7/X3	8737	200m	2.00	400.00					200	2.00	400.00
06/8/X3	8748	300m	2.00	600.00					500	2.00	1,000.00
07/8/X3					3771	400m	2.00	800.00	100	2.00	200.00

5 Summary

You should now be able to calculate:

- the cost issue of inventory for management accounting purposes using FIFO, LIFO and AVCO
- the closing values of inventory using FIFO, LIFO and AVCO
- the overhead cost per unit, using a cost per unit method, machine hour method and a labour hour method.

You should also be familiar with calculating the direct cost of a product in a manufacturing organisation taking into account the flow of inventory in the production process, what constitutes direct cost, manufacturing cost, cost of goods manufactured and cost of goods sold.

6 Further Test your understanding exercises

Test your understanding 13

Identify the correct inventory valuation method from the characteristic given by putting a tick in the relevant column of the table below.

Characteristic	FIFO	LIFO	AVCO
• Issues are valued at the most recent purchase cost.	☐	☐	☐
• Issues are valued at the oldest purchase cost.	☐	☐	☐
• Issues are valued at the average of the cost of purchases.	☐	☐	☐
• Inventory is valued at the most recent purchase cost.	☐	☐	☐
• Inventory is valued at the oldest purchase cost.	☐	☐	☐

Test your understanding 14

Adamkus Ltd has the following movements in a certain inventory item into and out of it stores for the month of March:

Date	Receipts		Issues	
	Units	Cost	Units	Cost
March 5	100	£200		
March 12	100	£250		
March 19	200	£600		
March 23			300	
March 27	400	£1,350		

Complete the table below for the issue and closing inventory values.

Method	Cost of issue on 23 March	Closing inventory at 31 March
FIFO		
LIFO		
AVCO		

Test your understanding 15

Identify the following statements as either true or false.

Statement	True	False
• FIFO costs issues of inventory at the oldest purchase price.	☐	☐
• AVCO values closing inventory at the oldest purchase price.	☐	☐
• LIFO costs issues of inventory at the oldest purchase price.	☐	☐

Test your understanding 16

Chiluba Ltd is costing a single product with the following cost details:

Variable costs per unit

Materials	£10
Labour	£5
Total fixed costs	£150,000

Complete the following total cost and unit cost table for a production level of 20,000 units.

Element	Total cost	Unit cost
Materials	£	£
Labour	£	£
Overheads	£	£
Total	£	£

Test your understanding 17

Complete the table below showing fixed costs, variable costs, total costs and unit cost at the different levels of production.

Units	Fixed costs	Variable costs	Total costs	Unit cost
1,000	£200,000	£5,000	£205,000	£205.00
2,000	£	£	£	£
3,000	£	£	£	£
4,000	£	£	£	£

Test your understanding 18

Reorder the following costs into a manufacturing account format:

	£
COST OF GOODS MANUFACTURED	**31,400**
MANUFACTURING COST	**29,400**
DIRECT COST	**20,000**
COST OF GOODS SOLD	**29,400**
DIRECT MATERIALS USED	12,800
Manufacturing overheads	9,400
Purchases of raw materials	12,000
Opening inventory of raw materials	2,800
Closing inventory of finished goods	(14,000)
Opening inventory of work in progress	8,400
Direct labour	7,200
Closing inventory of raw materials	(2,000)
Closing inventory of work in progress	(6,400)
Opening inventory of finished goods	12,000

Test your understanding answers

Test your understanding 1

Method	**Cost of issue on 19 June**	**Closing inventory at 30 June**
FIFO	£2,000	£3,100
LIFO	£2,200	£2,900
AVCO	£2,080	£3,020

Workings:

FIFO

- The issue will be made up of all 100 units from June 2, all 200 units from June 3 and 100 of those purchased on June 6 at a price of 1,200/200 = £6 per unit
- Cost of issue = £400 + £1,000 + (£100 × 6) = £2,000
- Total purchases = £400 + £1,000 + £1,200 + £2,500 = £5,100
- Closing inventory = £5,100 – £2,000 = £3,100

LIFO

- The issue will be made up of all 200 units from June 6 and all 200 units from June 3
- Cost of issue = £1,200 + £1,000 = £2,200
- Closing inventory = £5,100 – £2,200 = £2,900

AVCO

- Before June 19 we had bought a total of 500 units at a total cost of £400 + £1,000 + £1,200 = £2,600
- On average this works out at £2,600/500 = £5.20 per unit
- Thus the cost of the issue will be 400 × £5.20 = £2,080
- Closing inventory = £5,100 – £2,080 = £3,020

Test your understanding 2

Statement	True	False
FIFO values the closing inventory at £1,400.	☐	☑
LIFO costs the issue at £6,100.	☑	☐
AVCO costs the issue at £5,400.	☑	☐

Test your understanding 3

Statement	FIFO	LIFO	AVCO
The closing inventory is valued at £6,875.	☐	☐	☑
The issue of 3,750 units is costed at £18,750.	☑	☐	☐
The issue of 3,750 units is costed at £21,875.	☐	☑	☐

Test your understanding 4

Characteristic	FIFO	LIFO	AVCO
• Issues are valued at the most recent purchase cost.	☐	☑	☐
• Inventory is valued at the average of the cost of purchases.	☐	☐	☑
• Inventory is valued at the most recent purchase cost.	☑	☐	☐

Test your understanding 5

Statement	True	False
• FIFO costs issues of inventory at the most recent purchase price.	☐	☑
• AVCO costs issues of inventory at the oldest purchase price.	☐	☑
• LIFO costs issues of inventory at the oldest purchase price.	☐	☑
• FIFO values closing inventory at the most recent purchase price.	☑	☐
• LIFO values closing inventory at the most recent purchase price.	☐	☑
• AVCO values closing inventory at the latest purchase price.	☐	☑

Test your understanding 6

Element	Total cost	Unit cost
Materials	£60,000	£4.00
Labour	£75,000	£5.00
Overheads	£60,000	£4.00
Total	£195,000	£13.00

Test your understanding 7

Units	Fixed costs	Variable costs	Total costs	Unit cost
1,000	£60,000	£2,000	£62,000	£62.00
2,000	£60,000	£4,000	£64,000	£32.00
3,000	£60,000	£6,000	£66,000	£22.00
4,000	£60,000	£8,000	£68,000	£17.00

Test your understanding 8

Element	Total cost	Unit cost
Materials	£90,000	£6.00
Labour	£120,000	£8.00
Overheads	£90,000	£6.00
Total	£300,000	£20.00

Workings:

Materials

- This is a variable cost – unit cost is £6 (given)
- Total cost will be 15,000 × £6 = £90,000

Labour

- This is a variable cost – unit cost is £8 (given)
- Total cost will be 15,000 × £ = £120,000

Overheads

- Total cost is £90,000 (given)
- Total labour hours = 15,000 units × 2 hours = 30,000 hours
- Overhead rate per labour hour – £90,000 ÷ 30,000 hours = £3.00
- Overhead cost per unit is therefore 2 hours × £3.00/hour = £6.00

Test your understanding 9

Element	Total cost	Unit cost
Materials	£36,000	£3.00
Labour	£120,000	£10.00
Overheads	£120,000	£10.00
Total	£276,000	£23.00

Workings:

Materials

- This is a variable cost – unit cost is £3 (given)
- Total cost will be 12,000 × £3 = £36,000

Labour

- This is a variable cost – unit cost is £10 (given)
- Total cost will be 12,000 × £10 = £120,000

Overheads

- Total cost is £120,000 (given)
- Total machine hours = 12,000 units × 0.5 hours = 6,000 hours
- Overhead rate per machine hour = £120,000 ÷ 6,000 hours = £20
- Overhead cost per unit is therefore 0.5 hours × £20/hour = £10

Test your understanding 10

	£
Opening inventory of raw materials	14,000
Purchases of raw materials	60,000
Closing inventory of raw materials	(10,000)
DIRECT MATERIALS USED	64,000
Direct labour	36,000
DIRECT COST	**100,000**
Manufacturing overheads	47,000
MANUFACTURING COST	**147,000**
Opening inventory of work in progress	42,000
Closing inventory of work in progress	(32,000)
COST OF GOODS MANUFACTURED	**157,000**
Opening inventory of finished goods	60,000
Closing inventory of finished goods	(70,000)
COST OF GOODS SOLD	**147,000**

Test your understanding 11

	£
Prime cost	80,000
Manufacturing overheads	100,000
Total manufacturing costs	180,000
Cost of goods manufactured	182,000
Cost of goods sold	197,000

Prime cost = direct materials + direct labour

= £50,000 + £30,000

Manufacturing overheads = manufacturing expenses + indirect costs

= £82,000 + £12,000 + £6,000

Total manufacturing costs = prime cost + manufacturing overheads

= £80,000 + £100,000

Cost of good manufactured = manufacturing costs + opening WIP – closing WIP

= £180,000 + £7,000 - £5,000

Cost of goods sold = cost of goods manufactured + opening finished goods – closing finished goods

= £182,000 + £15,000 - £0

Test your understanding 13

Characteristic	FIFO	LIFO	AVCO
• Issues are valued at the most recent purchase cost.	☐	☑	☐
• Issues are valued at the oldest purchase cost.	☑	☐	☐
• Issues are valued at the average of the cost of purchases.	☐	☐	☑
• Inventory is valued at the most recent purchase cost.	☑	☐	☐
• Inventory is valued at the oldest purchase cost.	☐	☑	☐

Test your understanding 14

Method	Cost of issue on 23 March	Closing inventory at 31 March
FIFO	£750	£1,650
LIFO	£850	£1,550
AVCO	£787.50	£1,612.50

Workings:

FIFO

- The issue will be made up of all 100 units from March 5, all 100 units from March 12 and 100 of those purchased on March 19 at a price of £600/200 = £3 per unit
- Cost of issue = £200 + £250 + (100 × £3) = £750
- Total purchases = £200 + £250 + £600 + £1,350 = £2,400
- Closing stock = £2,400 – £750 = £1,650

LIFO

- The issue will be made up of all 200 units from March 19 and 100 units from March 12 at a price of £250/100 = £2.50 per unit
- Cost of issue = £600 + (100 × £2.50) = £850
- Closing stock = £2,400 – £850 = £1,550

AVCO

- Before March 23 we had bought a total of 400 units at a total cost of 200 + 250 + 600 = £1,050
- On average this works out at £1,050/400 = £2.625 per unit
- Thus the cost of the issue will be 300 × £2.625 = £787.50
- Closing stock = £2,400 – £787.5 = £1,612.50

Test your understanding 15

Statement	True	False
• FIFO costs issues of inventory at the oldest purchase price.	☑	☐
• AVCO values closing inventory at the oldest purchase price.	☐	☑
• LIFO costs issues of inventory at the oldest purchase price.	☐	☑

Test your understanding 16

Element	Total cost	Unit cost
Materials	£200,000	£10.00
Labour	£100,000	£5.00
Overheads	£150,000	£7.50
Total	£450,000	£22.50

Test your understanding 17

Units	Fixed costs	Variable costs	Total costs	Unit cost
1,000	£200,000	£5,000	£205,000	£205.00
2,000	£200,000	£10,000	£210,000	£105.00
3,000	£200,000	£15,000	£215,000	£71.67
4,000	£200,000	£20,000	£220,000	£55.00

Test your understanding 18

	£
Opening inventory of raw materials	2,800
Purchases of raw materials	12,000
Closing inventory of raw materials	(2,000)
DIRECT MATERIALS USED	12,800
Direct labour	7,200
DIRECT COST	**20,000**
Manufacturing overheads	9,400
MANUFACTURING COST	**29,400**
Opening inventory of work in progress	8,400
Closing inventory of work in progress	(6,400)
COST OF GOODS MANUFACTURED	**31,400**
Opening inventory of finished goods	12,000
Closing inventory of finished goods	(14,000)
COST OF GOODS SOLD	**29,400**

Labour costs

4

Introduction

This chapter considers labour costs in more detail.

ASSESSMENT CRITERIA
Recognise common costing techniques used in an organisation (1.2)
Identify sources of information about income and expenditure (1.4)
Calculate labour payments (2.2)
Calculate the direct cost of a product (2.5)

CONTENTS

1 Introduction

1.1 Labour costs

In this unit you need to understand and be able to explain methods of payment for labour to include basic rate (time rate), payment of overtime, payment of bonus and payment by piecework.

You will not be required to have knowledge of specific bonus schemes.

1.2 Direct and indirect labour

Just as materials can be classified as direct or indirect so too can labour costs, depending on the job of the employee.

Example 1

In a manufacturing organisation the factory workers who make the products would be direct labour whereas the factory supervisor would be an example of an indirect labour cost as although he is working in the factory he is not actually making any of the products.

Test your understanding 1

Identify the following statements as true or false by putting a tick in the relevant column of the table below.

Cost	True	False
Direct labour costs can be identified with the goods being made or the service being produced.	☐	☐
Indirect costs vary directly with the level of activity.	☐	☐

1.3 Calculating gross pay

There are two main methods of calculating the gross pay of employees:

- pay employees for the time spent at work (time related pay)
- pay employees for the work actually produced (output related pay).

In addition there may be bonus schemes to be incorporated. These are covered in more detail later in the chapter.

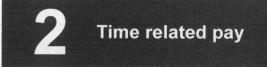

2 Time related pay

2.1 Time related pay

Employees paid under a time related pay method are paid for the hours that they spend at work regardless of the amount of production or output that they achieve in that time. Time related pay employees can be split into two types, **salaried employees** and **hourly rate employees**.

2.2 Salaried employees

Definition

A **salaried employee** is one whose gross pay is agreed at a fixed amount for a period of time whatever hours that employee works in that period.

This might be expressed as an annual salary such as £18,000 per year or as a weekly rate such as £269.50 per week.

Each organisation will have a set number of hours that are expected to be worked each week, for example a standard working week of 37.5 hours, and salaried employees will be expected to work for at least this number of hours each week.

However if the salaried employee works for more than the standard number of hours for the week then the employment agreement may specify that overtime payments are to be made for the additional hours.

2.3 Hourly rate employees

Definition

An **hourly rate employee** is one who is paid a set hourly rate for each hour that he works.

These employees are paid for the actual number of hours of attendance in a period, usually a week. A rate of pay will be set for each hour of attendance.

2.4 Overtime

Definition

Overtime is the number of hours worked by an employee which is greater than the number of hours set by the organisation as the working week.

It is common that employees that work overtime are paid an additional amount per hour for those extra hours.

2.5 Overtime premium

Definition

Overtime premium is the amount over and above the normal hourly rate that employees are paid for overtime hours.

Example 2

An employee's basic week is 40 hours at a rate of pay of £8 per hour. Overtime is paid at 'time and a half'. The employee works a 45-hour week. What is the total gross pay for this employee for the week?

	£
Basic hours 40 × £8	320.00
Overtime 5 × £12	60.00
	380.00

The overtime payment can be split between the basic rate element and the overtime premium:

	£
Basic pay 5 × £8	40.00
Overtime premium 5 × £4	20.00
	60.00

Test your understanding 2

Singh Ltd pays a time-rate of £12 per hour to its direct labour for a standard 35 hour week. Any of the labour force working in excess of 35 hours is paid an overtime rate of £15 per hour.

Calculate the gross wage for the week for the workers in the table below.

Worker	Hours worked	Basic wage £	Overtime £	Gross wage £
J. Patel	35			
D. Smith	38			
S. O'Leary	42			

3 Output related pay

Output related pay is also known as 'payment by results' or 'piecework'. This is a direct alternative to time related pay.

Definition

Payment by results or piecework is where a fixed amount is paid per unit of output achieved irrespective of the time spent.

3.1 Advantages of payment by results

As far as an employee is concerned, payment by results means that they can earn whatever they wish within certain parameters. The harder they work and the more units they produce the higher the wage they will earn.

From the employer's point of view higher production or output can also be encouraged with a system of differential piecework (see later in chapter).

3.2 Problems with payment by results

There are two main problems associated with payment by results. One is the problem of accurate recording of the actual output produced. The amount claimed to be produced determines the amount of pay and, therefore, is potentially open to abuse unless it can be adequately supervised. A system of job sheets and checking of job sheets needs to be in place.

The second problem is that of the maintenance of the quality of the work. If the employee is paid by the amount that is produced then the temptation might be to produce more units but of a lower quality.

For these reasons basic piecework systems are rare in practice – variations of these systems are used instead.

Test your understanding 3

Stizgt Ltd uses a piecework method to pay labour in one of its factories. The rate used is 90p per unit produced.

Calculate the gross wage for the week for the workers in the table below.

Worker	**Units produced in week**	**Gross wage £**
S. McHenry	200 units	
D. Weaver	320 units	
S. Hasina	250 units	

3.3 Piece rate with guarantee

A **piece rate with guarantee** gives the employee some security if the employer does not provide enough work in a particular period. The way that the system works is that if an employee's earnings for the amount of units produced in the period are lower than the guaranteed amount then the guaranteed amount is paid instead.

Test your understanding 4

Fernando is paid £3.00 for every unit that he produces but he has a guaranteed wage of £28.00 per eight hour day. In a particular week he produces the following number of units:

Monday	12 units
Tuesday	14 units
Wednesday	9 units
Thursday	14 units
Friday	8 units

Calculate Fernando's wage for this week.

4 Bonus schemes

Bonuses may be paid to employees for a variety of reasons. An individual employee, a department, a division or the entire organisation may have performed particularly well and it is felt by the management that a bonus is due to some or all of the employees.

4.1 Basic principle of bonuses

The basic principle of a bonus payment is that the employee is rewarded for any additional income or savings in cost to the organisation. This may be, for example, because the employee has managed to save a certain amount of time on the production of a product or a number of products. This time saving will save the organisation money and the amount saved will tend to be split between the organisation and the employee on some agreed basis. The amount paid to the employee/employees is known as the bonus.

4.2 Method of payment

The typical bonus payable will often depend on the method of payment of the employee. The calculation and payment of bonuses will differ for salaried employees, employees paid by results and employees paid on a time rate basis.

4.3 Bonus cap

Employees may also be paid a bonus depending on the level of output they produce. Where output exceeds a certain level, a bonus per unit may be paid. For example, if output is greater than 350 units in a given week, then a bonus of £0.20 per unit may be applied. This incentivises workers to achieve higher levels of output. However, companies will often place a '**cap**' on the bonus, so that it is only paid up to a certain level of output. Continuing our previous example, the bonus may be capped at 500 units. Therefore, a bonus will be paid for all units produced over 350 units, but not more than 500 units. If an employee was to produce 550 units, for example, then the bonus would only be paid for units 351-500 (and not for units 501-550).

Example 3

A company has a production target of 400 units for each production employee per week. Any excess production is rewarded by a bonus of £6 per unit, capped at a maximum production of 480 units.

An employee who produces 420 units in the week will earn a bonus on the 20 additional units they produce:

Bonus = 20 units x £6 = £120

An employee who produces 500 units in the week will only earn a bonus on the units up to 480. Any units above the bonus cap will not earn a bonus (so units 481-500):

Bonus = 80 units x £6 = £480

An employee who produces 400 units will not earn a bonus. The bonus is only paid for any units made **in excess** of 400, and so the first unit to earn a bonus will be unit 401.

Test your understanding 5

Meidani Ltd uses a time-rate method with bonus to pay its direct labour in one of its factories. The time-rate used is £10 per hour and a worker is expected to produce 6 units an hour, anything over this and the worker is paid a bonus of £2 per unit.

Calculate the gross wage for the week for the workers in the table below.

Worker	Hours worked	Units produced	Basic wage £	Bonus £	Gross wage £
J. Klestil	35	220			
C. Zemin	35	205			
J. Chirac	40	240			

Test your understanding 6

Identify the labour payment method by putting a tick in the relevant column of the table below.

Payment method	Time-rate	Piece-rate	Time-rate plus bonus
Labour is paid based on the production achieved.	☐	☐	☐
Labour is paid extra if an agreed level of output is exceeded.	☐	☐	☐
Labour is paid according to hours worked.	☐	☐	☐

Test your understanding 7

Identify one **advantage** for each labour payment method by putting a tick in the relevant column of the table below.

Payment method	**Time-rate**	**Piece-rate**	**Time-rate plus bonus**
Assured level of remuneration for employee.	☐	☐	☐
Employee earns more if they work more efficiently than expected.	☐	☐	☐
Assured level of remuneration and reward for working efficiently.	☐	☐	☐

Test your understanding 8

A company has a production target of 350 units for each production employee in a given week. Any excess production is rewarded with a bonus of £7 per unit, capped at a maximum production of 400 units.

Identify whether the bonus calculations for the following employees are correct or incorrect:

Bonus calculation	**Correct**	**Incorrect**
Employee 1 produces 340 units and earns a bonus of £0.	☐	☐
Employee 2 produces 350 units and earns a bonus of £7.	☐	☐
Employee 3 produces 370 units and earns a bonus of £140.	☐	☐
Employee 4 produces 420 units and earns a bonus of £490.	☐	☐

5 Sources of information

5.1 Documentation and procedures to record labour costs

When an employee joins an organisation it must record details of the employee, their job and pay. This is done by the personnel department in the individual employee's personnel record.

Details that might be kept about an employee are as follows:

- full name, address and date of birth
- personal details such as marital status and emergency contact name and address
- National Insurance number
- previous employment history
- educational details
- professional qualifications
- date of joining organisation
- employee number or code
- clock number issued
- job title and department
- rate of pay agreed
- holiday details agreed
- bank details if salary is to be paid directly into bank account
- amendments to any of the details above (such as increases in agreed rates of pay)
- date of termination of employment (when this takes place) and reasons for leaving.

5.2 Employee record of attendance

On any particular day an employee may be at work, on holiday, absent due to sickness or absent for some other reason. A record must be kept of these details for each day.

This information about an employee's attendance will come from various sources such as clock cards, time sheets, job sheets, and job cards.

6 Summary

In this chapter we looked at different ways of calculating a labour cost. Make sure you can distinguish between time-rate, piece-rate and bonus schemes.

7 Further Test your understanding exercises

Test your understanding 9

Karimov Ltd pays a time-rate of £10 per hour to its direct labour for a standard 37 hour week. Any of the labour force working in excess of 37 hours is paid 'time and a half'.

Calculate the gross wage for the week for the workers in the table below.

Worker	Hours worked	Basic wage £	Overtime £	Gross wage £
M. Khan	42			
D. Murphy	37			
K. Ng	40			

Test your understanding 10

Gibson plc uses a piecework method to pay labour to make clothing in one of its factories. The rate used is £2.50 per garment completed.

Calculate the gross wage for the week for the workers in the table below.

Worker	Units produced in week	Gross wage £
H. Potter	100 units	
T. Riddle	130 units	
S. Snape	175 units	

Test your understanding 11

Leona is paid £5.00 for every unit that she produces but she has a guaranteed minimum wage of £25.00 per day.

Calculate Leona's wage for this week by filling in the following table:

Day	**Units produced**	**Gross wage** £
Monday	4 units	
Tuesday	6 units	
Wednesday	9 units	
Thursday	3 units	
Friday	8 units	
Total	30 units	

Test your understanding 12

Legolas Ltd uses a time-rate method with bonus to pay its direct labour in one of its factories. The time-rate used is £12 per hour and a worker is expected to produce 10 units an hour, anything over this and the worker is paid a bonus of £1 per unit.

Calculate the gross wage for the week for the workers in the table below.

Worker	**Hours worked**	**Units produced**	**Basic wage** £	**Bonus** £	**Gross wage** £
L. Aragon	37	375			
T. Ent	35	360			
K. Theodin	42	410			

Test your understanding answers

Test your understanding 1

Cost	True	False
Direct labour costs can be identified with the goods being made or the service being produced.	☑	☐
Indirect costs vary directly with the level of activity.	☐	☑

Test your understanding 2

Worker	Hours worked	Basic wage £	Overtime £	Gross wage £
J. Patel	35	420	0	420
D. Smith	38	420	45	465
S. O'Leary	42	420	105	525

Test your understanding 3

Worker	Units produced in week	Gross wage £
S. McHenry	200 units	180.00
D. Weaver	320 units	288.00
S. Hasina	250 units	225.00

Test your understanding 4

Fernando would be paid £176.

Working:

Total weekly wage

	£
Monday (12 × 3)	36
Tuesday (14 × 3)	42
Wednesday (guarantee)	28
Thursday (14 × 3)	42
Friday (guarantee)	28
	176

The payment of a guaranteed amount is not a bonus for good work but simply an additional payment required if the amount of production is below a certain level.

Test your understanding 5

Worker	Hours worked	Units produced	Basic wage £	Bonus £	Gross wage £
J. Klestil	35	220	350	20	370
C. Zemin	35	205	350	0	350
J. Chirac	40	240	400	0	400

Working:

- Basic wage = £10 × hours worked.
- In 35 hours we would expect 35 × 6 = 210 units.
  J Klestil exceeded this by 10 units, giving a bonus of 10 × 2 = £20.
  C. Zemin did not, so received no bonus.
- In 40 hours we would expect 40 × 6 = 240 units.
  J. Chirac did not exceed this, so received no bonus.

Test your understanding 6

Payment method	Time-rate	Piece-rate	Time-rate plus bonus
Labour is paid based on the production achieved.	☐	☑	☐
Labour is paid extra if an agreed level of output is exceeded.	☐	☐	☑
Labour is paid according to hours worked.	☑	☐	☐

Test your understanding 7

Payment method	Time-rate	Piece-rate	Time-rate plus bonus
Assured level of remuneration for employee.	☑	☐	☐
Employee earns more if they work more efficiently than expected.	☐	☑	☐
Assured level of remuneration and reward for working efficiently.	☐	☐	☑

Test your understanding 8

Bonus calculation	Correct	Incorrect
Employee 1 produces 340 units and earns a bonus of £0.	☑	☐
Employee 2 produces 350 units and earns a bonus of £7.	☐	☑
Employee 3 produces 370 units and earns a bonus of £140.	☑	☐
Employee 4 produces 420 units and earns a bonus of £490.	☐	☑

Employee 1 has not reached the production target of 350 units and so will not earn a bonus.

Employee 2 has reached the target, but not produced any units in excess of the target. The bonus will be paid for units 351 upwards.

Employee 3 has produced 20 units more than the production target, and so will earn a bonus of 20 x £7 = £140.

Employee 4 has produced 70 units more than the production target. However, the bonus is capped at 400 units, and so the bonus will only be paid on units 351-400 (50 units). The maximum bonus payable will therefore be 50 x £7 = £350.

Test your understanding 9

Worker	Hours worked	Basic wage £	Overtime £	Gross wage £
M. Khan	42	370	75	445
D. Murphy	37	370	0	370
K. Ng	40	370	45	415

Test your understanding 10

Worker	Units produced in week	Gross wage £
H. Potter	100 units	250.00
T. Riddle	130 units	325.00
S. Snape	175 units	437.50

Test your understanding 11

Day	Units produced	Gross wage £
Monday	4 units	25
Tuesday	6 units	30
Wednesday	9 units	45
Thursday	3 units	25
Friday	8 units	40
Total	30 units	165

Test your understanding 12

Worker	Hours worked	Units produced	Basic wage £	Bonus £	Gross wage £
L. Aragon	37	375	444	5	449
T. Ent	35	360	420	10	430
K. Theodin	42	410	504	0	504

Budgeting and variances

5

Introduction

This chapter looks briefly at budgeting before focussing on variances and how they can be used to help control an organisation.

ASSESSMENT CRITERIA
Compare actual and budgeted costs and income (3.1)
Apply exception reporting to identify significant variances (3.2)

CONTENTS

1 Budgeting

1.1 Introduction

In this unit you need to have a brief knowledge of budgeting as an aid to planning and control but this need only be at a basic level.

You will not be required to explain the nature of budgeted costs in any great detail, but will be required to identify budgeted costs and to compare with actual costs by using variances.

1.2 What is budgeting?

Budgets set out the costs and revenues that are expected to be incurred or earned in future periods.

For example, if you are planning to take a holiday, you will probably have a budgeted amount that you can spend. This budget will determine where you go and for how long.

Most organisations prepare budgets for the business as a whole. The following budgets may also be prepared by organisations:

- Departmental budgets.
- Functional budgets (for sales, production, expenditure and so on).
- Statements of profit or loss/income statements (in order to determine the expected future profits).
- Cash budgets (in order to determine future cash flows).

1.3 Budgetary control

As stated in Chapter 1, the main reason for budgeting is to help managers control the business.

The budget contains a mixture of what you think will happen and what you intend to make happen.

For example, suppose we think we will be able to sell 100 units in June (a sales forecast) and therefore plan to make 100 units in May (a production budget). This means we need to buy 200 kg of material X at an expected cost of £5 per kg (a materials purchases budget).

This then gives a benchmark against which we can evaluate actual performance.

For example, what if we only sold 90 units, or used 210 kg of material or it cost £5.50/kg not £5.

Any difference or 'variance' can then be investigated to identify the cause. Once we know this we can take appropriate action.

For example, if the price of materials was higher because our normal supplier put their prices up, then we could consider trying to find another supplier.

1.4 Other reasons for budgeting

Other reasons for budgeting include the following:

- **Authorisation**

  A budget may act as a formal authorisation to a manager to spend a given amount on specified activities.

- **Forecasting**

  Forecasting refers to the prediction of events over which little or no control is exercised. Some parts of all budgets are, therefore, based on forecasts.

- **Planning**

  Planning is an attempt to shape the future by a conscious effort to influence those factors which are open to control.

- **Communication and co-ordination**

  Budgets communicate plans to managers responsible for carrying them out. They also ensure co-ordination between managers of sub-units so that each is aware of the others' requirements.

- **Motivation**

  Budgets are often intended to motivate managers to perform in line with organisational plans and objectives.

- **Evaluation**

  The performance of managers and organisational units is often evaluated by reference to budgetary targets.

2 Identifying budgeted costs

2.1 Introduction

Within this unit you will need to be able to calculate total and unit costs at different activity levels.

2.2 Cost behaviour

When calculating budgeted costs remember to distinguish between variable costs and fixed costs

- Fixed costs will remain constant for each activity level.
- Variable costs will increase in line with activity levels.

Example 1

Complete the table below showing budgeted fixed costs, variable costs, total costs and unit cost at the different possible budgeted levels of production.

Units	Fixed costs	Variable costs	Total costs	Unit cost
100	400	200	600	6.00
200				
300				

Solution

Units	Fixed costs	Variable costs	Total costs	Unit cost
100	400	200	600	6.00
200	400	400	800	4.00
300	400	600	1,000	3.33

Notes: You may recall doing similar calculations in Chapter 1.

- Fixed costs do not change.
- To get variable costs either
  - (a) simply prorate – e.g. to go from 100 to 300 units the volume has trebled, so treble the cost: 3 × 200 = £600, or
  - (b) first calculate the variable cost per unit = 200/100 = £2 per unit. This can be used to work out other variable costs, so for 300 units the variable cost will be 300 × 2 = £600.
- Total costs are simply the sum of fixed and variable.

To get the unit cost, divide the total cost by the number of units. So for 200 units the unit cost = £800/200 = £4 per unit.

Test your understanding 1

Complete the table below showing budgeted fixed costs, variable costs, total costs and unit cost at the different budgeted levels of production.

Units	Fixed costs	Variable costs	Total costs	Expected unit cost
1,000	£2,400	£600	£3,000	£3.00
2,000				
3,000				
4,000				

Test your understanding 2

Moussa Ltd is budgeting for the costs of a single product which has the following cost details:

Variable costs per unit:

- Materials £5 per unit
- Labour £8 per unit
- Total fixed costs £60,000

Complete the following budgeted total cost and unit cost table for a production level of 30,000 units.

Element	**Total cost** £	**Unit cost** £
Materials		
Labour		
Overheads		
Total		

Test your understanding 3

Barak Ltd makes a single product and has estimated the following expected costs for a budgeted production level of 12,000 units:

- Materials 3,600 kg at £5 per kg
- Labour 600 hours at £12 per hour
- Overheads £60,000

Complete the table below to show the expected unit cost at the production level of 12,000 units.

Element	**Unit cost** £
Materials	
Labour	
Overheads	
Total	

3 Variances

3.1 What is a variance?

The difference between actual and expected (or budgeted) cost is known as a variance.

- A **favourable** variance ('Fav') is when the actual cost is lower than expected and
- An **adverse** variance ('Adv') is when actual cost is higher than expected.

3.2 How to calculate a variance

For Elements of Costing the only calculations required will be a comparison of actual to expected costs or revenues.

Example 2

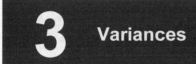

Fujimori Ltd has produced a performance report detailing budgeted and actual material cost for last month.

Calculate the amount of the variance and then determine whether it is adverse or favourable by putting a tick in the relevant column of the table below.

Cost type	Budget £	Actual £	Variance £	Adv.	Fav.
Materials	24,500	26,200		☐	☐

Solution

Cost type	Budget £	Actual £	Variance £	Adv.	Fav.
Materials	24,500	26,200	1,700	☑	☐

Notes:

- Variance = 26,200 – 24,500 = £1,700
- The variance is adverse as **the actual cost is higher** than budgeted.

Example 3

Sushi Ltd has produced a performance report detailing budgeted and actual sales revenue for last year.

Calculate the amount of the variance and then determine whether it is adverse or favourable by putting a tick in the relevant column of the table below.

Cost type	Budget £	Actual £	Variance £	Adv.	Fav.
Sales	17,500	16,950		☐	☐

Solution

Cost type	Budget £	Actual £	Variance £	Adv.	Fav.
Sales	17,500	16,950	550	☑	☐

Notes:

- Variance = £17,500 – £16,950 = £550
- The variance is adverse as the **actual revenue is lower** than budgeted.

Test your understanding 4

Kagame Ltd has produced a performance report detailing budgeted and actual cost for last month.

Calculate the amount of the variance for each cost type and then determine whether it is adverse or favourable by putting a tick in the relevant column of the table below.

Cost type	Budget £	Actual £	Variance £	Adv.	Fav.
Materials	56,000	49,500		☐	☐
Labour	64,000	65,200		☐	☐
Overheads	150,000	148,500		☐	☐

Test your understanding 5

Identify the following statements as being true or false by putting a tick in the relevant column of the table below.

Statement	True	False
A variance is the difference between budgeted and actual cost.	☐	☐
A favourable variance means budgeted costs are greater than actual costs.	☐	☐
An adverse variance means you have made a saving compared to budgeted costs.	☐	☐

3.3 Evaluating the significance of a variance

Management do not want to waste time investigating small variances, so will set criteria for deciding what makes a variance large enough to report and investigate.

For example:

- 'Only investigate variances bigger than £500'
- 'Only investigate variances bigger than 5% of budget'

If using a percentage measure then the amount of the variance that exceeds the cut-off percentage is known as the 'discrepancy'.

Example 4

Antrobus Ltd has produced a performance report detailing budgeted and actual material cost for last month. Any variance in excess of 10% of budget is deemed to be significant and should be reviewed.

Calculate the amount of the variance and then determine whether it is significant by putting a tick in the relevant column of the table below.

Cost type	Budget £	Actual £	Variance £	Significant	Not significant
Labour	5,600	5,200		☐	☐

Solution

Cost type	**Budget** £	**Actual** £	**Variance** £	**Significant**	**Not significant**
Labour	5,600	5,200	400	☐	☑

Notes:

- Variance = £5,200 – £5,600 = £400
- As a % of budget this gives (400/5,600) × 100% = 7.1%, which is less than 10%, so the variance is deemed not significant.

Test your understanding 6

Guterres Ltd has produced a performance report detailing budgeted and actual cost for this month. Any variance in excess of 5% of budget is deemed to be significant and should be reported to the relevant manager.

Examine the variances in the table below and indicate whether they are significant or not by putting a tick in the relevant column.

Cost type	**Budget** £	**Variance** £	**Significant**	**Not significant**
Direct materials	26,000	1,200	☐	☐
Direct labour	35,000	2,000	☐	☐
Production overheads	15,000	1,100	☐	☐
Selling costs	2,000	90	☐	☐

Test your understanding 7

Jonas Ltd has produced a performance report detailing budgeted and actual cost for this month. Any variance in excess of 5% of budget is deemed to be significant and should be reported to the relevant manager.

Examine the variances in the table below, calculate the variance as a percentage of budget, rounded to two decimal places, and then determine whether they are significant (S) or Not Significant (NS) in the relevant column.

Cost type	Budget £	Variance £	%	S or NS
Direct materials	24,000	1,600		
Direct labour	45,000	1,800		
Production overheads	19,000	1,750		
Selling costs	1,900	70		

3.4 Reporting variances

Actions and their consequences should be traced to the person responsible. This may give the impression of 'laying the blame', but it is equally possible to award praise (and remunerate accordingly).

Responsibility accounting is a system which recognises various decision centres within a business and traces costs (and possibly revenues) to the individual managers who are primarily responsible for making decisions about the items in question.

You may be asked in your assessment on the appropriateness of reporting a particular variance to a suggested manager.

For example, reporting sales variances to the sales manager would make sense, as he/she is then in the right position to be able to act on such information. If an adverse variance has occurred this period, it makes sense to try to ensure that it does not occur again next period.

It should be noted that a decision could result in either a favourable or an adverse variance, and that the overall picture should be the basis for subsequent action.

Example 5

A purchasing manager is looking to place an order to buy fresh direct materials. Instead of ordering from the usual supplier, she is made aware that a different supplier will charge a much lower price than the business usually pays. If this then results in a favourable direct material cost variance, the purchasing manager has acted well and should be praised accordingly.

However, if the reason for the low price is that the materials are of much lower quality, with the result that there is much greater than usual wastage, this might produce overall an adverse variance. Accordingly, the purchasing manager should not buy from that supplier again.

Test your understanding 8

Identify the following statements as being true or false by putting a tick in the relevant column of the table below.

Statement	True	False
The variance for the direct material cost of Department A should be reported to the purchasing manager.	☐	☐
The variance for the direct labour cost of Department B should be reported to the production manager of Department A.	☐	☐
The variance for sales revenue should be reported to the sales manager.	☐	☐
The adverse variance for the direct labour cost of Department A should be reported to the Human Resources manager, who agreed pay rises for all production staff.	☐	☐

4 Summary

In this chapter we looked briefly at budgeting, how to calculate budget costs and the basics of variance analysis. We also looked at the significance of variances, and to whom they should be reported.

5 Further Test your understanding exercises

Test your understanding 9

Ben Ali Ltd has produced a performance report detailing budgeted and actual cost for last month.

Calculate the amount of the variance for each cost type and then determine whether it is adverse or favourable by putting a tick in the relevant column of the table below.

Cost type	Budget £	Actual £	Variance £	Adv.	Fav.
Sales	175,000	176,850		☐	☐
Labour	15,000	14,950		☐	☐
Overheads	120,600	120,000		☐	☐

Test your understanding 10

Identify the following statements as being true or false by putting a tick in the relevant column of the table below.

Statement	True	False
A variance is the difference between actual and budgeted cost.	☐	☐
A variance is the average of actual and budgeted cost.	☐	☐
A favourable variance means this cost element would reduce profit compared to budget.	☐	☐
An adverse variance means you have made a saving compared to budgeted costs.	☐	☐

Test your understanding 11

Ionatana Ltd has produced a performance report detailing budgeted and actual material cost for last month. Any variance in excess of 6% of budget is deemed to be significant and should be reviewed.

Calculate the amount of the variance and then determine whether it is significant by putting a tick in the relevant column of the table below.

Cost type	Budget	Actual	Variance	Significant?	
	£	£	£	Yes	No
Direct labour	10,000	9,500		☐	☐
Direct materials	13,000	15,200		☐	☐
Production overheads	24,000	25,120		☐	☐
Administration costs	35,000	32,400		☐	☐
Selling and distribution costs	45,000	49,260		☐	☐

Test your understanding 12

You have been provided with the following information related to last month's performance.

	Budgeted £	Actual £
Labour costs	145,000	162,400

In addition to this, you are told that:

- Variances in excess of 5% of budget, and that are greater than £5,000, are significant and should be reported to the department manager.
- Adverse variances in excess of 10% of budget, and that are greater than £20,000, are significant and should be reported to the department director.

Calculate the following:

(a) The variance on labour costs.

(b) The percentage labour cost variance to TWO decimal places.

(c) Whether the variance is adverse or favourable.

(d) Whether the variance is significant or not.

(e) Who (if anyone) the variance should be reported to.

Test your understanding answers

Test your understanding 1

Units	Fixed costs	Variable costs	Total costs	Expected unit cost
1,000	£2,400	£600	£3,000	£3.00
2,000	£2,400	£1,200	£3,600	£1.80
3,000	£2,400	£1,800	£4,200	£1.40
4,000	£2,400	£2,400	£4,800	£1.20

Test your understanding 2

Element	Total cost £	Unit cost £
Materials	150,000	5
Labour	240,000	8
Overheads	60,000	2
Total	450,000	15

Test your understanding 3

Element	Unit cost £
Materials	1.50
Labour	0.60
Overheads	5.00
Total	7.10

Notes:

- To get material costs per unit, either
  (a) calculate the total material cost (3,600 × £5 = 18,000) and divide this by the number of units: 18,000 ÷ 12,000 = £1.50 per unit, or
  (b) first calculate the usage per unit = 3,600/12,000 = 0.3 kg per unit. The cost per unit is then 0.3 kg at £5 per kg = £1.50.
- To get labour costs per unit, either
  (a) calculate the total labour cost (600 × £12 = £7,200) and divide this by the number of units: £7,200 ÷ 12,000 = £0.60 per unit, or
  (b) first calculate the time per unit – 600/12,000 = 0.05 hours per unit. The cost per unit is then 0.05 hours at £12 per hour = £0.60.
- To get the overhead unit cost, divide the total cost by the number of units = £60,000/12,000 = £5 per unit.

Test your understanding 4

Cost type	Budget £	Actual £	Variance £	Adv.	Fav.
Materials	56,000	49,500	6,500	☐	☑
Labour	64,000	65,200	1,200	☑	☐
Overheads	150,000	148,500	1,500	☐	☑

Test your understanding 5

Statement	True	False
A variance is the difference between budgeted and actual cost.	☑	☐
A favourable variance means budgeted costs are greater than actual costs.	☑	☐
An adverse variance means you have made a saving compared to budgeted costs.	☐	☑

Test your understanding 6

Cost type	Budget £	Variance £	Significant	Not significant
Direct materials	26,000	1,200	☐	☑
Direct labour	35,000	2,000	☑	☐
Production overheads	15,000	1,100	☑	☐
Selling costs	2,000	90	☐	☑

Workings:

- Materials (1,200/26,000) × 100 = 4.6%
- Labour (2,000/35,000) × 100 = 5.7%
- Overheads (1,100/15,000) × 100 = 7.3%
- Selling costs (90/2,000) × 100 = 4.5%

Test your understanding 7

Cost type	Budget £	Variance £	%	S or NS
Direct materials	24,000	1,600	6.67	S
Direct labour	45,000	1,800	4.00	NS
Production overheads	19,000	1,750	9.21	S
Selling costs	1,900	70	3.68	NS

Test your understanding 8

Statement	True	False
The variance for the direct material cost of Department A should be reported to the purchasing manager.	☑	☐
The variance for the direct labour cost of Department B should be reported to the production manager of Department A.	☐	☑
The variance for sales revenue should be reported to the sales manager.	☑	☐
The adverse variance for the direct labour cost of Department A should be reported to the Human Resources manager, who agreed pay rises for all production staff.	☑	☐

Test your understanding 9

Cost type	Budget £	Actual £	Variance £	Adv.	Fav.
Sales	175,000	176,850	1,850	☐	☑
Labour	15,000	14,950	50	☐	☑
Overheads	120,600	120,000	600	☐	☑

Test your understanding 10

Statement	True	False
A variance is the difference between actual and budgeted cost.	☑	☐
A variance is the average of actual and budgeted cost.	☐	☑
A favourable variance means this cost element would reduce profit compared to budget.	☐	☑
An adverse variance means you have made a saving compared to budgeted costs.	☐	☑

Test your understanding 11

Cost type	Budget	Actual	Variance	Significant?	
	£	£	£	Yes	No
Direct labour	10,000	9,500	500	☐	☑
Direct materials	13,000	15,200	2,200	☑	☐
Production overheads	24,000	25,120	1,120	☐	☑
Administration costs	35,000	32,400	2,600	☑	☐
Selling and distribution costs	45,000	49,260	4,260	☑	☐

Test your understanding 12

(a) Variance on labour costs = £162,400 – £145,000 = £17,400

(b) Percentage labour cost variance = variance/budget x 100

= £17,400/£145,000 x 100 = 12.00%

(c) Actual labour costs were greater than budget, therefore the variance is adverse.

(d) The variance percentage is greater than 5% of budget, and therefore will be considered significant.

(e) The variance percentage is in excess of 10% of budget and is adverse. However, it is not in excess of £20,000 and so the second bullet does not apply. The variance therefore needs to be reported to the department manager.

MOCK ASSESSMENT

1 Mock Assessment Questions

TASK 1.1

(a) (i) Select TWO of the descriptions used when classifying costs by function from the list below by dragging them into the answer box. (2 marks)

Answer		
	Variable	Fixed
	Direct	Indirect
	Cost of sales	Distribution costs

(ii) Complete the following sentences using the drop-down lists. (2 marks)

Costs that are fixed up to any level of activity are known as ▽

Drop-downs:

variable costs.
stepped costs.
fixed costs.
semi-variable.

When a manufacturing business classifies costs by element for production, electricity costs would be recorded as ▽

Drop-downs:

labour.
materials.
overheads.

(b) Identify whether the following statements are true or false. **(2 marks)**

Statement	True	False
Financial accounts must be presented in a format specified by regulation.		
Management accounts may include future forecasts.		

Happy Toys Ltd, a traditional wooden toy manufacturer, uses an alphanumeric coding system to allocate costs.

(c) (i) Code the following transactions for the project, using the table below. Each transaction should have a six character code. **(2 marks)**

Activity	Code	Sub-class	Sub code	Transaction	Code
Sales	SAL	Rocking horses	100	Leather costs	
		Teddy Bears	200	Teddy bear sales	
Production	PRO	Wood	110		
		Wages	210		
		Leather	310		
Administration	ADM	Telephone	220		
		Wages	216		

(ii) Identify whether the following statements are true or false using the drop-down list below. **(2 marks)**

A manufacturing account shows the cost of goods manufactured during an accounting period.

∇
True
False

In a manufacturing account the direct cost total excludes manufacturing overheads.

∇
True
False

TASK 1.2

(a) Identify whether the following statements are true or false. **(2 marks)**

Statement	True	False
AVCO uses the oldest values of purchases to value closing inventories.		
LIFO uses the most recent values of purchases to value inventory issues.		

(b) (i) Identify the labour costing methods described below using the drop down list. **(1 mark)**

Labour costs are calculated by multiplying a basic rate by the number of items produced, supplemented by an additional amount if production exceeds a certain level. ▽

Drop-downs

Piece rate
Time rate
Piece rate with bonus
Piece rate with guarantee
Time rate with overtime

(ii) Identify whether the following statement is true or false using the drop-down list. **(1 mark)**

Direct labour is never salaried. ▽

True
False

(c) Identify TWO ways in which information on historic costs is used by clicking on the left-hand box and matching it to the appropriate right-hand boxes. **(2 marks)**

Uses for historic costs

To prepare annual accounts
To value inventory
To classify cost elements
To help set unit sales prices
To help management plan labour needs

(d) Identify TWO examples of cost centres and ONE example of a profit centre for a manufacturing business from the items below by dragging them into the appropriate answer box. (3 marks)

Cost centre	**Profit centre**

Quality control department	Sales division
Administration costs	HR department
Production director wages	Raw materials

(e) In a manufacturing business that is machine intensive the most appropriate overhead absorption method would be: (1 mark)

	∇

Drop-down

Per unit
Per labour hour
Per machine hour

TASK 1.3

Fantail Ltd uses the first in first out (FIFO) of inventory control.

One receipt and one issue of raw material SL3 were made during the first half of May. These are shown in the inventory record below:

(a) Complete the inventory record below for the receipt and issue of SL3 during May, and calculate closing balance at 13 May.

The cost per litre entries should be completed in pounds (£) to THREE decimal places. (6 marks)

Date	Receipt			Issue			Balance	
	Quantity (litres)	Cost per litre (£)	Total cost (£)	Quantity (litres)	Cost per litre (£)	Total cost (£)	Quantity (litres)	Total cost (£)
Balance at 1 May							1,000	10,500
10 May	6,000		62,400					
13 May				3,000			4,000	

(b) Identify the cost of the issue on 13 May and closing inventory balance if Fantail Ltd had used the weighted average cost (AVCO) or last in first out (LIFO) methods instead. (4 marks)

Using AVCO the cost of the issue would be £ ∇ and the closing inventory balance: £ ∇

Issue (£)	Closing inventory (£)
31,200	41,400
31,243	41,657
31,500	41,700

Using LIFO the cost of the issue would be £ ∇ and the closing inventory balance: £ ∇

Issue (£)	Closing inventory (£)
31,200	41,400
31,243	41,657
31,500	41,700

TASK 1.4

A company pays its employees a basic rate of £12 per hour for a 35 hour working week (Monday to Friday).

Any overtime during the week is paid at time and a half (basic pay + 50%).

Any weekend working is paid at double time (2 × basic pay).

(a) **Calculate the basic pay, overtime and gross pay for the week for an employee working the hours shown below.**

All hours worked are paid at basic rate with the overtime premiums being the increased pay only. **(4 marks)**

Hours worked Monday to Friday	Hours worked at the weekend	Basic pay £	Overtime premium earned during week £	Overtime premium earning at weekends £	Gross pay £
36	10				

The company has a production target of 600 units for each production employee. Any excess production is rewarded by a bonus of £5 per unit, capped at a maximum production of 650 units.

(b) **Identify whether the bonus calculations for the following employees are correct or incorrect.** **(4 marks)**

Bonus calculation	Correct	Incorrect
Employee 1 produces 560 units and earns a bonus of £0.		
Employee 2 produces 600 units and earns a bonus of £5.		
Employee 3 produces 620 units and earns a bonus of £100.		
Employee 4 produces 660 units and earns a bonus of £300.		

TASK 1.5

Digitech Ltd is considering how to cost the various products it makes. It needs to decide on the overhead absorption basis it will use. The methods it is considering are:

- machine hour basis
- labour hour basis
- per unit basis

(a) Complete the table below to show the three overhead absorption rates that Digitech Ltd could use. Show your calculations to two decimal places. (3 marks)

	Machine hour	Labour hour	Unit
Overheads (£)	360,000	360,000	360,000
Activity	120,000	30,000	50,000
Absorption rate (£)			

(b) Complete the table below to calculate the total unit cost of product GT3. Use each of the three overhead absorption rates you calculated in (a). Show your calculations to two decimal places. (6 marks)

Each unit of GT3 takes 6 minutes of machine time and 20 minutes of labour time to produce.

	Machine hour (£)	Labour hour (£)	Unit (£)
Direct cost	27.50	27.50	27.50
Overheads			
Total unit cost			

(c) Which of the three overhead recovery methods would best be suited to a production line where items are hand made by highly skilled craftsmen / women? (1 mark)

	∇
Machine hours	
Labour hours	
Per unit	

TASK 1.6

A manager needs to understand how the costs of the company's single product change at different output levels.

(a) Complete the table below to separate out the variable and fixed costs of the product. (6 marks)

Note: You should use the high-low method to divide the total costs into their variable and fixed elements.

Units	Total costs £	Variable costs £	Fixed costs £
4,000	21,000		
6,500	26,000		
9,000	31,000		

(b) Identify the correct cost behaviour for the four costs shown below. (4 marks)

Cost behaviour	Fixed	Variable	Semi-variable	Step-fixed
The cost consists of a part that stays the same and a part that changes with the output level.				
The cost is fixed for a limited output range and then increases.				
The unit cost is the same whatever the output level.				
The total cost is the same whatever the output level.				

TASK 1.7

Good life Ltd has the following information for its last quarter:

	£
Materials costs:	
Materials forming part of product	45,000
Materials not forming part of product	4,000
Labour costs:	
Labour working on production	15,000
Labour supporting work on production	20,000
Factory indirect expenses	22,000

Relevant inventory changes were as below:

	£
Work in progress:	
Opening	5,000
Closing	11,000
Finished goods:	
Opening	12,000
Closing	25,000

Complete the table below to show Good Life Ltd's cost structure for the last quarter. **(8 marks)**

Cost structure for the last quarter	£
Direct materials cost	
Direct labour costs	
Manufacturing overhead	
Total manufacturing cost	
Cost of goods manufactured	
Cost of goods sold	

TASK 1.8

All ten production employees in a company are paid a basic £10 per hour for a 30 hour working week (Monday to Friday).

Any overtime during the week is paid at time and a quarter (basic pay + 25%).

Any weekend working is paid at double time (2 × basic pay).

(a) Calculate the basic pay, overtime and gross pay for the week for each employee working the hours shown below. (Note: All hours worked are paid at basic rate with the overtime premiums being the increased pay only). (4 marks)

Hours worked Monday to Friday	Hours worked at the weekend	Basic pay £	Overtime premium earned during week £	Overtime premium earned at weekends £	Gross pay £
36	8				

Each employee has a production target of 3,000 units per month. All production in excess of this is rewarded by a bonus of £0.10 per additional unit. Last month 3,600 units were produced per employee.

(b) Complete the following sentence. (1 mark)

Last month each employee was paid a bonus of: £ [ ]

The gross pay for each employee was the same as you calculated in (a) in each of the four weeks last month.

(c) Complete the following sentence. (1 mark)

Last month the total pay including bonuses for ALL ten production employees was: £ [ ]

(d) (i) Calculate the total cost and cost per unit of last month's production.

(ii) Calculate what these figures would have been if production had increased to 37,440 units. (8 marks)

Notes:

1 The direct labour cost for the production of 36,000 units is your figure calculated in part (c) above.

2 Calculate the costs per unit to three decimal places.

Units produced and sold	36,000	37,440
	£	£
Variable costs:		
Direct Materials	61,920	
Direct labour		
Fixed costs:		
Manufacturing overheads	27,500	
Total cost		
Cost per unit		

TASK 1.9

The production cost centre of a factory spent £900 less on raw materials that was budgeted and £800 more than was budgeted on wages.

(a) (i) Complete the table below to show the actual expense and identify whether the variance was adverse or favourable. **(4 marks)**

	Budgeted expense £	Actual expense incurred £	Adverse/ Favourable
Raw materials	6,700		∇
Wages	5,450		∇

Drop down

Adverse
Favourable

(ii) Identify whether the following statement is true or false by using the tick boxes below. **(1 mark)**

Statement	True	False
A company that has an adverse variance on sales has received less income than budgeted.		

You are reviewing the performance of the research department. The variance on research costs was 12% over the budgeted figure.

(b) Complete the table below to show the variance and actual expense, and identify whether the variance was adverse or favourable. (3 marks)

	Budgeted expense £	Variance £	Adverse/ Favourable	Actual expense £
Research costs	125,000		∇	

Drop down

Adverse
Favourable

TASK 1.10

You have been asked to provide information on the company performance report for the month. The budgeted and actual figures have already been summarised in the information below.

	Budgeted £	Actual £
Marketing costs	125,000	132,000

(a) (i) Calculate the variance on marketing costs. (1 mark)

£ [ ]

(ii) Calculate the percentage marketing costs variance to TWO decimal places. (1 mark)

[ ] %

(iii) Identify whether the variance is favourable or adverse using the drop-down list. (1 mark)

Drop down

Adverse
Favourable

You have been provided with variance information by your assistant.

Reporting policies state that

- Variances in excess of 5% of budget, and that are greater than £500, are significant. They should be reported to the department manager.
- Adverse variances in excess of 10% of budget, and that are greater than £1,000, are significant. They should be reported to the department director.
- Any variances in excess of 20% of budget, and that are greater than £2,000, are significant. They should be reported to the department director.

(b) Complete the table below to show each variance percentage. Identify whether the variance is significant or not, and who (if anyone) the information should be reported to.

Percentages should be to TWO decimal places. (9 marks)

	Budgeted income/ expense £	Actual income/ expense incurred £	Variance £	Variance as % of budget	Significant/ not significant	Report to
Sales	245,000	276,000	31,000		∇	∇
Telephone	12,700	12,850	150		∇	∇
Production wages	106,500	134,800	28,300		∇	∇

LH Drop downs	
	Significant
	Not significant

RH drop downs	
	Departmental manager
	Not required
	Department director

2 Mock Assessment Answers

TASK 1.1

(a) (i) Select TWO of the descriptions used when classifying costs by function from the list below by dragging them into the answer box. **(2 marks)**

Answer
Cost of sales
Distribution costs

(ii) Complete the following sentences using the drop-down lists. **(2 marks)**

Costs that are fixed up to any level of activity are known as	**fixed costs.**
When a manufacturing business classifies costs by element for production, electricity costs would be recorded as	**overheads.**

(b) Identify whether the following statements are true or false. **(2 marks)**

Statement	True	False
Financial accounts must be presented in a format specified by regulation.	X	
Management accounts may include future forecasts.	X	

(c) (i) Code the following transactions for the project, using the table below. Each transaction should have a six character code. (2 marks)

Activity	Code	Sub-class	Sub code	Transaction	Code
Sales	SAL	Rocking horses	100	Leather costs	**PRO310**
		Teddy Bears	200	Teddy bear sales	**SAL200**
Production	PRO	Wood	110		
		Wages	210		
		Leather	310		
Administration	ADM	Telephone	220		
		Wages	216		

(ii) Identify whether the following statements are true or false using the drop-down list below. (2 marks)

A manufacturing account shows the cost of goods manufactured during an accounting period.

True

In a manufacturing account the direct cost total excludes manufacturing overheads.

True

TASK 1.2

(a) Identify whether the following statements are true or false. (2 marks)

Statement	True	False
AVCO uses the oldest values of purchases to value closing inventories.		X
LIFO uses the most recent values of purchases to value inventory issues.	X	

(b) (i) Identify the labour costing methods described below using the drop down list. (1 mark)

Labour costs are calculated by multiplying a basic rate by the number of items produced, supplemented by an additional amount if production exceeds a certain level. ∇

Piece rate with bonus

(ii) Identify whether the following statement is true or false using the drop-down list. (1 mark)

Direct labour is never salaried. ∇

False

(c) Identify TWO ways in which information on historic costs is used by clicking on the left-hand box and matching it to the appropriate right-hand boxes. (2 marks)

To prepare annual accounts
To value inventory

(d) Identify TWO examples of cost centres and ONE example of a profit centre for a manufacturing business from the items below by dragging them into the appropriate answer box. (3 marks)

Cost centre	Profit centre
Quality control department	Sales division
HR department	

(e) In a manufacturing business that is machine intensive the most appropriate overhead absorption method would be: (1 mark)

Per machine hour

TASK 1.3

(a) Complete the inventory record below for the receipt and issue of SL3 during May, and calculate closing balance at 13 May.

The cost per litre entries should be completed in pounds (£) to THREE decimal places. (6 marks)

Date	Receipt			Issue			Balance	
	Quantity (litres)	Cost per litre (£)	Total cost (£)	Quantity (litres)	Cost per litre (£)	Total cost (£)	Quantity (litres)	Total cost (£)
1 May							1,000	10,500
10 May	6,000	**10.400**	62,400				**7,000**	**72,900**
13 May				3,000	**10.433**	**31,300**	4,000	**41,600**

(b) Identify the cost of the issue on 13 May and closing inventory balance if Fantail Ltd had used the weighted average cost (AVCO) or last in first out (LIFO) methods instead. (4 marks)

Using AVCO the cost of the issue would be £	**31,243**	and the closing inventory balance: £	**41,657**
Using LIFO the cost of the issue would be £	**31,200**	and the closing inventory balance: £	**41,700**

TASK 1.4

(a) Calculate the basic pay, overtime and gross pay for the week for an employee working the hours shown below.

All hours worked are paid at basic rate with the overtime premiums being the increased pay only. (4 marks)

Hours worked Monday to Friday	Hours worked at the weekend	Basic pay £	Overtime premium earned during week £	Overtime premium earning at weekends £	Gross pay £
36	10	**552**	**6**	**120**	**678**

(b) Identify whether the bonus calculations for the following employees are correct or incorrect. (4 marks)

Bonus calculation	Correct	Incorrect
Employee 1 produces 560 units and earns a bonus of £0.	X	
Employee 2 produces 600 units and earns a bonus of £5.		X
Employee 3 produces 620 units and earns a bonus of £100.	X	
Employee 4 produces 660 units and earns a bonus of £300.		X

TASK 1.5

(a) Complete the table below to show the three overhead absorption rates that Digitech Ltd could use. Show your calculations to two decimal places. (3 marks)

	Machine hour	Labour hour	Unit
Overheads (£)	360,000	360,000	360,000
Activity	120,000	30,000	50,000
Absorption rate (£)	**3.00**	**12.00**	**7.20**

(b) Complete the table below to calculate the total unit cost of product GT3. Use each of the three overhead absorption rates you calculated in (a). Show your calculations to two decimal places. (6 marks)

Each unit of GT3 takes 6 minutes of machine time and 20 minutes of labour time to produce.

	Machine hour (£)	Labour hour (£)	Unit (£)
Direct cost	27.50	27.50	27.50
Overheads	**0.30**	**4.00**	**7.20**
Total unit cost	**27.80**	**31.50**	**34.70**

(c) Which of the three overhead recovery methods would best be suited to a production line where items are hand made by highly skilled craftsmen / women? (1 mark)

Labour hours

TASK 1.6

(a) Complete the table below to separate out the variable and fixed costs of the product. (6 marks)

Note: You should use the high-low method to divide the total costs into their variable and fixed elements.

Units	Total costs £	Variable costs £	Fixed costs £
4,000	21,000	**8,000**	**13,000**
6,500	26,000	**13,000**	**13,000**
9,000	31,000	**18,000**	**13,000**

(b) Identify the correct cost behaviour for the four costs shown below. (4 marks)

Cost behaviour	Fixed	Variable	Semi-variable	Step-fixed
The cost consists of a part that stays the same and a part that changes with the output level.			X	
The cost is fixed for a limited output range and then increases.				X
The unit cost is the same whatever the output level.		X		
The total cost is the same whatever the output level.	X			

TASK 1.7

Complete the table below to show Good Life Ltd's cost structure for the last quarter. (8 marks)

Cost structure for the last quarter	£
Direct materials cost	**45,000**
Direct labour costs	**15,000**
Manufacturing overhead	**46,000**
Total manufacturing cost	**106,000**
Cost of goods manufactured	**100,000**
Cost of goods sold	**87,000**

TASK 1.8

(a) Calculate the basic pay, overtime and gross pay for the week for each employee working the hours shown below. (Note: All hours worked are paid at basic rate with the overtime premiums being the increased pay only). (4 marks)

Hours worked Monday to Friday	Hours worked at the weekend	Basic pay £	Overtime premium earned during week £	Overtime premium earned at weekends £	Gross pay £
36	8	**440**	**15**	**80**	**535**

(b) Complete the following sentence. (1 mark)

Last month each employee was paid a bonus of: £ **60**

(c) Complete the following sentence. (1 mark)

Last month the total pay including bonuses for ALL ten production employees was: £ **22,000**

(d) (i) Calculate the total cost and cost per unit of last month's production.

(ii) Calculate what these figures would have been if production had increased to 37,440 units. (8 marks)

Units produced and sold	**36,000**	**37,440**
	£	£
Variable costs:		
Direct Materials	61,920	**64,397**
Direct labour	**22,000**	**22,880**
Fixed costs:		
Manufacturing overheads	27,500	**27,500**
Total cost	**111,420**	**114,777**
Cost per unit	**3.095**	**3.066**

TASK 1.9

(a) (i) Complete the table below to show the actual expense and identify whether the variance was adverse or favourable. (4 marks)

	Budgeted expense £	**Actual expense incurred** £	**Adverse/ Favourable**
Raw materials	6,700	**5,800**	**Favourable**
Wages	5,450	**6,250**	**Adverse**

(ii) Identify whether the following statement is true or false by using the tick boxes below. (1 mark)

Statement	**True**	**False**
A company that has an adverse variance on sales has received less income than budgeted.	**X**	

(b) Complete the table below to show the variance and actual expense, and identify whether the variance was adverse or favourable. (3 marks)

	Budgeted expense £	**Variance** £	**Adverse/ Favourable**	**Actual expense** £
Research costs	125,000	**15,000**	**Adverse**	**140,000**

TASK 1.10

(a) (i) Calculate the variance on marketing costs. (1 mark)

£ **7,000**

(ii) Calculate the percentage marketing costs variance to TWO decimal places. (1 mark)

5.60 %

(iii) Identify whether the variance is favourable or adverse using the drop-down list. (1 mark)

Adverse

(b) Complete the table below to show each variance percentage. Identify whether the variance is significant or not, and who (if anyone) the information should be reported to.

Percentages should be to TWO decimal places. (9 marks)

	Budgeted income/ expense £	**Actual income/ expense incurred** £	**Variance** £	**Variance as % of budget**	**Significant/ not significant**	**Report to**
Sales	245,000	276,000	31,000	**12.65**	**Significant**	**Manager**
Telephone	12,700	12,850	150	**1.18**	**Not significant**	**Not required**
Production wages	106,500	134,800	28,300	**26.57**	**Significant**	**Director**

INDEX